COMPASS

ALSO BY PENELOPE YORKE
    Compass Companion Workbook
    Compass Reflection Journals

COMPASS

The Journey of the Soul
from Egypt to the Promised Land

Penelope V. Yorke

Copyright © 2015 Penelope V. Yorke

All rights reserved. No part of this book may be reproduced, distributed or transmitted in any form or by any means, electronic or mechanical, including photocopying, recording, or by any information storage and retrieval system, without prior written permission from the publisher except for the use of brief quotations in a book review.

Publisher: PCS Resources: PCS@penelopeyorke.com

"Excerpts taken from the *Metaphysical Bible Dictionary*. Used with permission of Unity, www.unity.org."

"All Scripture quotations in this publication are from THE MESSAGE. Copyright © by Eugene H. Peterson 1993, 1994, 1995, 1996, 2000, 2001, 2002. Used by permission of Tyndale House Publishers, Inc."

ISBN 978-0-9863896-2-7 (paperback)
ISBN 978-0-9863896-7-2 (digital)
ISBN 978-0-9863896-1-0 (audiobook)

Cover Art and Interior Art: Neil Hague, www.NeilHague.com

Editor: Nancy Buffington, www.BoiseSpeakWell.com

Interior Layout: Kevin Mullani, www.TruPublishing.com

With God, My Friend,
Without Whom
I Would Cease to Exist.

To My Spirit,
You Came With a Big Agenda.
I Accept Our Truth.

To My Parents,
Michael Yorke & Doreen Yorke.
Transitioned but Never Forgotten.

Contents

Chapter 1

    The Journey Begins 1

Chapter 2

    Following the Path 10

Chapter 3

    Beginning Your Dialogue 18

Chapter 4

    Discovering Your Soul... 26

Chapter 5

    Creation Becomes the Purpose..................................... 35

Chapter 6

    Crossing the Jordan River... 42

Chapter 7

    Stepping Stones in the Jordan..51

Chapter 8

    Entering Canaan...59

Chapter 9

    You Too Are God 66

Chapter 10

    The Land Called Egypt..75

Chapter 11

    The Voyage over the Sea 85

Chapter 12

    Becoming One with Silence 90

Chapter 13

    Different Aspects of Yourself 99

Chapter 14

    Filling the Empty Space 109

Chapter 15

    Challenging Your Fears 119

Chapter 16

    The Land of Milk and Honey 128

Chapter 17

    Adverse Thinking 138

Chapter 18

    Becoming the Christ 149

Chapter 19

    Learning How to Relate to You 163

Chapter 20

    Where Are You? 174

Chapter 21

    Every Master Takes the Journey 185

Chapter 22

    The Illusions to Be Surrendered 196

Chapter 23

    The Greatest Illusion 201

Chapter 24

    What Is It for Me to Do? 211

Chapter 25

    Cultivating a Self-Relationship 218

Chapter 26

    Why Take the Journey? 228

Poem - The Journey 231

From the Author 233

Notes 237

Bibliography 240

Decide to take a journey into
the unknown depths of your soul.

1

The Journey Begins

WHEN YOU HEAR THE WORD *Egypt**, what images come to mind? Do you envision pyramids, pharaohs, sand, or gold? These are some of the symbols associated with ancient *Egypt*. For most of us, we picture the country in Northern Africa. But I am referring to another Egypt: a stage of spiritual development in consciousness. There are six stages of spiritual development on the journey of the soul: Egypt, Red Sea, Wilderness, Jordan River, Promised Land and Christ Consciousness. In the Egypt stage of development we too have symbols

* The word *Egypt*, when in italics, refers to the country. When not italicized, the word Egypt refers to a stage of spiritual development. The stages of spiritual development are universal to every religion or spiritual practice.

that we can identify with, such as an education, wealth, an attractive appearance, a home, and a car. This stage of development, and the *Egypt* of old, both epitomize a materialistic period of existence. "Egypt signifies the darkness of ignorance, obscurity . . . and we often think of it as referring to the subjective or subconscious mind. We also refer to Egypt as the flesh consciousness, sense consciousness, or material consciousness."[1]

The Egypt of biblical times was a place abundant in material wealth. Egyptians were rich in glitzy things like gold, jewelry, and architecture. There was, of course, another side to life. They enslaved the Hebrew people, whose job it was to sustain their lifestyle. The slaves' lives were not filled with material riches, although they toiled so others might have them. Their riches were of a different nature. Their riches were dreams that they looked to be fulfilled in the future. They tolerated as best as they could their present moment, living for a time called "when" in the future. In their minds, the future became the time when their dreams would be fulfilled: a Promised Land of sorts. How many of us do this now? I still do sometimes. We voluntarily leave now, the present moment, and enter into the land of when.

When I was in the Egypt stage of development, the interests I pursued there seemed to fulfill me. The process of striving for goals, and obtaining them, gave me great satisfaction. These pursuits gave me something to do in life. There was never a question of what I should do. I was part of the collective consciousness of America that *knew* what one was supposed to do.

You went to school to get a degree. You got yourself a nice place to live, and you bought yourself the best car you could afford. You competed to obtain the best paying job possible. You worked yourself up in the ranks until you got your own office. You were certain you had made it when you received your first business cards. You worked very hard for every three percent raise that you got.

The Journey Begins

I look back fondly on the time that I spent there, for the preoccupations were simple and straightforward. I did not have time for introspection, because I was so busy *doing* in the world.

When we are in the Egypt stage of development, we are focused on obtaining material goals. As soon as we accomplish one goal, we work hard to accomplish the next. Until something happened—one day I looked up and found no more immediate goals to pursue. The goals I had accomplished thus far left me feeling unfulfilled and empty. My storehouse was filled with outer things. I pondered what was next in my life: I wondered what I was supposed to do, who I was supposed to be. According to society, I should be married with children, making as close to six figures as possible, weighing x amount, have long hair, a trendy wardrobe, a flashy car, a large house, a big bank account, and stocks. It is the American Dream. Who defines these as the criteria for success? We do, when we are in Egypt.

When I remember my youth, I think back on all the ways I tried to escape the now, the living in the present moment. My most favorite forms of escape were books and daydreaming. I was always told as a child that I lived in a dream world. I often wondered what was wrong with that, for my dream world was always so much better than my real one. In my dream world, I was loved for no reason other than the fact that I existed. There was no lack of anything: money, love, time, or dreams. Books taught me that there was a life possible that was different than the one I was living.

I miss daydreaming. My dreams were precious friends. They offered the only way out of the present-day life I was living as a child. Dreaming helped me to transcend my parents' version of the life I was living. I will cherish the dreams of my childhood always as useful tools that helped me survive it.

You can imagine my dismay in my twenties, when I realized it was time for me to stop daydreaming. The life that I lived in my head had become my primary life, and my physical life had become secondary. The problem when this happens is that you start incorporating people from your physical life into the imaginary life in your head. You create roles that you assign to people, and they act them out in your mind. My imaginary life featured villains, heroes, and always the same victim: me. Someone else always did something to me—life, co-workers, parents, family, friends, myself, evil, fate, and so on and so on. I call these the "poor-me" years.

During this time I sought traditional therapy. I went to a psychologist to tell me what was wrong with me, why I was so chronically unhappy. I had to find the source of the despair. This course of action helped me for a while. The feedback I received gave me tools to manage all of my experiences up until to that point in my life. Therapy was a good experience for me. I needed to revisit my childhood with an adult consciousness in order to heal myself from the wounds and scars that remained in my psyche.

Therapy was not an easy process, but a useful one. There came a time, after prodding and poking around for several years in my painful childhood memories, that I became more focused on my life in the present moment. Yes, I could now recall most of my childhood experiences, and worked through them. But now what? I wanted to know how I could find happiness and be at peace in the now. This is the point where traditional therapy and I parted ways. I had become Moses.

I remember watching a biblical movie on the TNT cable network, on the life of Joseph. You know, the one with the dream coat. Joseph, sold into a life of slavery by his brothers, is representative of the time in our lives when we betray ourselves by abandoning our spiritual pursuits for material ones, and when we sell our dreams short.

Joseph was entrusted with the job of filling the storehouses in *Egypt* with grain for seven years. He had learned through a divinely inspired dream that a time would come when the nation would exhaust its outer resources.² The only way to survive would be to use the resources stored for such a time. Like Joseph, when all of our outer resources have been exhausted, the only way left to receive nourishment is to go inside—inside of ourselves—and use the resources found there.

It was time to leave Egypt and its preoccupation with the outer, and intuitively seek out the inner. My journey had begun, although I did not know where it would lead. I had to take about a million of my troubling thoughts, the remaining burdens I still carried after therapy, and my hopes and dreams to go on a quest seeking that elusive thing called happiness. My willingness and commitment to see this journey through spurred me to take a leap of faith into the unknown.

I call this leap of faith "crossing the Red Sea." What started me on my journey was at first a simple desire for better, for more, and for fulfillment. This fervent desire enabled me to cross over the Red Sea of my fears. I intuitively knew I would find what I was looking for. This feeling of *knowingness* served as a source of comfort to me on the long journey ahead. Moses had come to lead me to the Promised Land.

Moses is leading you when a new conscious spiritual thought system comes to the forefront of your awareness. Your indwelling guide, Moses serves now as the predominant thought system in your consciousness. Moses comes in order to lead you out of material bondage in Egypt, and to lead you into the Wilderness. But first you must cross over the Red Sea of fear, worry, and doubt that besiege you. The Red Sea is "the boundary line where we sacrifice every tie that binds us to the past."³ Crossing the Red Sea is the initial leap of faith you must take when beginning your spiritual journey. Old thought patterns, the bonds from Egypt that held you in captivity, must now be crossed over in consciousness.

This rite of passage is exemplified by Moses, who led about one million people through the Red Sea despite their fears and doubts. Those who crossed the Red Sea embarked on the journey of the soul courageously. The Red Sea served as the median point between their old and new lives.

Our Moses consciousness has come to lead about one million or more of our own adverse thoughts through the Red Sea of our fears. But first we must find an opening in our thoughts—an opening that parts in order for us to reach higher ground, where an evolved way of thinking emerges. We are pioneers seeking to enlarge our territories in the areas of life such as relationships, jobs, family, money, health, and so forth.

It is now time to start making demands on Pharaoh. Pharaoh represents the consciousness of the old, dominant thought system based on the material, which has ruled your life up until now.[4] Pharaoh is also known by another name: ego. Your Moses consciousness is propelled to the forefront of your awareness by the emerging connection to your spirit. Thus, Moses begins to battle Pharaoh for supremacy as the sole leader of your thoughts.

When you agree to answer the call from your spirit to journey it feels like a force, larger than you, is spurring you to take action. This force can best be described as a call to action, resonating like a horn deep inside of you. The sound of the horn gets louder, until it becomes the predominant force guiding your actions. A sense of urgency comes from a place within you, demanding that you take action of some sort. If, because of fear, you wait too long to follow your spirit's call to action, there is a strong possibility that your heart will begin to harden. It may become closed, impenetrable to spirit. The opportunity to move to a higher place in consciousness may pass you by. The fear of watching this very thing happen to me was the deciding factor that made me act.

This battle occurred in me when I decided to give up my job and enter the unknown in hopes of finding fulfillment. At first the notion of quitting my job cold turkey seemed impossible. But every day that I delayed in answering my soul's call to move, I paid the price. I felt an intense, almost painful ache from deep within me, which refused to abate

The Journey Begins

until I surrendered to its wishes. Moses was demanding that I let his people go. The fate-filled time approached; I left my cushy, well-paying job to seek out the unknown. I began a journey of the soul.

Two weeks later, I had a serious car accident that left me without a vehicle and bedridden in pain. I mainly had bruises and lacerations. A nurse told me that my seat belt saved my life. The company I had left in order to take my journey sent me a beautiful tropical arrangement of flowers. That made my guilt about leaving my job even worse. I almost went back to Egypt then. The ties that bound me to Egypt were hard to break.

Have you ever noticed that when you decide to leave a situation you have outgrown, people do their best to keep you stuck there? Sometimes they even inundate you with kindness. This can be a dangerous trap. I experienced this when I left my job, but I was determined to see my journey through to the end, wherever it led me. My body healed. I was able to do occasional freelance jobs at home. I was basically fine financially, but I was struggling in a new romantic relationship. The honeymoon period, which makes up the first three to six months of any new relationship, was over. Reality set in hard.

Three months later, my father had a massive heart attack. After I spent a month by his side, watching him come close to dying numerous times, he passed away. I witnessed every major organ in his body shut down. It was official. I was in the valley, or what I refer to as the Wilderness. It was the darkest place I have ever been in. I wanted to die, but I knew I had to will myself to live. My romantic relationship was in shambles. My father, the person I had loved most was now gone in physical form.

By this time I was also financially broke. Because of the accident, I didn't have a car. But worst of all, I had no sense of direction or purpose. I had no real desire to remain on this planet. I could not believe that this was where my journey—which I had voluntarily chosen to undertake—

had brought me. In my old life in Egypt, everything basically had been fine. Was this where the desire for more and fulfillment had left me—seemingly with nothing?

COMPASS

Once you leave Egypt, if you become homeless and penniless, lose family and friends, and lose all material prestige in the eyes of the world, who are you?

2

Following the Path

THE PURPOSE OF THE WILDERNESS is for you to develop an authentic and close relationship with God. When I crossed over the sea of my doubts I entered the Wilderness. My former minister at Unity Center of Light once explained the Wilderness succinctly: "It is the place you go to be only with God."

It is quiet in the Wilderness; there are few outer distractions. You are typically stranded in some form or another. For some, it may be in a form of illness. For me, I was stranded in one location, the place where I lived, because I did not have a car anymore and had nowhere to go each day. I was also stranded emotionally due to my grief and pain over my father's passing, my failing relationship, and fears about my life. "The Wilderness represents in individual consciousness the multitude of undisciplined and uncultivated thoughts."[3]

In the Wilderness, your Moses consciousness teaches you the requirements necessary for spiritual development. Your unruly thoughts, which unbeknownst to you fuel your behavior, must be tamed and brought under spiritual control. Since you are newly out of Egypt, the desire to go back to familiar land will have you always looking over your shoulder to what was. You are tempted by what could be again. In the Wilderness, Moses represents the aspect of you that is the executor of laws in this new land where your consciousness has arrived. You stay in the Wilderness phase of development typically for two to three years, when you undertake the journey of the soul for the first time.

In the Wilderness phase of spiritual development, the primary directive you learn is to become completely dependent on God. God gives you all necessary sustenance in the Wilderness phase, making you dependent on a source other than yourself for basic survival. Any thoughts of doubt, which may make you try storing away provisions for tomorrow, will prove futile. You will be given, on a day-to-day basis, what you need in order to survive for that day alone. All attempts to provide your own sustenance by outer means will fail at this stage in your life. The job of Moses in the Wilderness is to train you, by limiting certain behaviors that prevent you from developing spiritually.

Every day in the Wilderness seemed like the previous one. I would wake up and be disappointed to be awake. I would try to go back to sleep as many times as possible until it was at least noon—or, if I was lucky, two o'clock. You can get a headache from too much sleep; not many people know this. When it became headache time, I knew that I must awake. I did all of the normal routine things one does upon awakening. But at some point during the day, after trying to distract myself with music, television, or reading, it was time for me to be with God.

Sometimes I prayed, which I have learned is simply talking with God. But more times than not, my prayers were in silence. I would simply be still and lie down, allowing his presence to wash over me. It felt like balm for the many emotional wounds I had sustained in Egypt. Each day I would let out a little bit more of the poison inside of me. It was as though the presence of God was emptying it out of me. At this stage in my life, I was full of poison. I used to visualize it as garbage being burned; a self-help book said this was a useful exercise. But this visualization did not really help me. The poison trickled out of me slowly and methodically.

I did many spiritual things during this period: I read the right books, spoke the right mantras, wrote in journals, and watched spiritual shows on TV. I went to spiritual conferences, to church, and more. But the only thing I found that really healed me was being still and quiet for countless hours in the presence of God.

I am not going to mislead you: this is not a pretty stage. But for me it was a necessary one. Your experience does not have to be as dark as mine was. Not only was I going through the Wilderness experience, I was also having a spiritual epiphany referred to as the "Dark Night of the Soul." During this time, I knew I was not depressed in the clinical sense. I knew what I was going through was related to a spiritual epiphany of some sort.

When you are in the Wilderness, the only question that preoccupies your mind is "when?" "When will this experience end?" is the question you will ask yourself the most. The answer: no time soon. The Wilderness experience seems like an endless journey through pain, tedium, and boredom. No amount of begging and pleading and prayer can end this experience before its due time. The only way to expedite the process is to go through the darkest parts within you, without delay. Exposing your darkness to light is the only way you can heal. Do the required work without hesitation. Do it diligently and wholeheartedly.

You cannot stop to despair about the amount of work involved. I know that it seems never ending. It also seems to be cyclical. Each time you are sure you have sufficiently learned your lesson, but it comes around again in the guise of a new experience. It takes you a while to remember that you have been here before, and to remember what you learned here before. If I have already learned it, you wonder to yourself, why it is coming up again? It is because there was something more for you to learn or to understand more fully.

The Wilderness is the place where many spiritual lessons are taught to you. In the Wilderness you learn coping and survival skills of a spiritual nature. The lessons learned here will aid you for the rest of your life. A great battle wages in this place of isolation: your illusion of having power and control in your life, versus the truth that the only real power is God's power. God will not wrest your illusions away from you. Instead, he waits for the time when you willingly place them down. The Wilderness is the place where you learn that you can do nothing on your own. This is one of the hardest lessons to learn. Up until now, you could still hold onto the illusion that you could bring about your desires through perseverance, hard work, determination, or sheer desperation.

But in the Wilderness you learn that nothing you attempt outwardly will work. Do not resist recognizing that your outer attempts to reestablish order and control in your life fail to work for a very important spiritual reason. If you choose to continue fighting against what is occurring spiritually, you will suffer much longer and more deeply than you need to. For instance, when you are in the Wilderness, you do not have a job. If you can embrace that there is a higher reason for this state of affairs, and do nothing outwardly to change it, your time in the Wilderness will be better spent.

There are those who will try to buck the system. They insist on sending out resumes, pounding the pavement looking for a job. The constant rejection eats away at their soul. If they manage by sheer force of will to find a job, it will not last for long; this depresses them even more. The denial stage can go on for years without them understanding that there is a spiritual reason for the place they find themselves.

You must force and discipline yourself to be still when you are in this land. One of the first lessons to be learned in the Wilderness stage of development is that of obedience. You are learning to obey the circumstances that have been sent to you, to force you to become still. Any attempt to hold onto the illusion that your own efforts can change the circumstances that brought you to this place will simply lengthen your stay in the Wilderness. When you give up fighting the state of the current circumstances of your life, you typically sink into a deep depression and a self-pity mode. You beat up on yourself; you see yourself and your life as a failure. You are forced to battle feelings of suicide, which overwhelm you at times. Life seems hopeless and dark, because the material terms by which you used to define success—possessions, a job—are now gone. According to the world, you are a loser and a failure.

You must determine for yourself whether or not this is the truth. Can you sense that there is something else going on? Can you feel that there is a higher power involved here? All of this is happening to you quite purposefully. It is neither random failure nor bad luck. As you detach from the self that you most identified with up until this point—your human personality—you discover an amazing thing. There is a part of you that now emerges, that you are in contact with for the first time. This awakened part of you is indifferent to the challenging circumstances in your life. It does not feel ashamed or embarrassed by what is occurring in your life. Secretly, you feel that none of what is occurring has anything to do with you anyway—not the *real* you. The truth is that it does not.

There emerges in the Wilderness a clear delineation between the mask that you wear in the world and the truth of your being. One identity starts to give way to the other. The real you, which you have started to identify with in the Wilderness, is your soul. It is unaffected by the outer circumstances in your life. You learn that you are not less of anything because you lack a job, money, or any other material possessions. These criteria of success were defined by others, and by your ego. At this time, you must let go of false beliefs on what constitutes success.

This is when the journey in the Wilderness becomes interesting. The more time you spend in silence in the Wilderness, the better you feel. You start to learn that a whole new you exists, and it is not concerned with the outer events in your life. The main characteristic of this new self seems to be a preoccupation with silence. Silence, to your soul, appears to be the one thing that liberates it from the pain it is experiencing. It is the only thing that provides comfort.

Silence is not something that is comfortable to be in—especially not at first. It seems boring, and you feel an initial resistance to being still mentally and physically. But as you first go through this feeling of resistance, no matter how much time it takes, you will arrive at a place where you begin to welcome the silence. You even start to need and depend on it. Being around other people too much, or doing too much in this period, agitates your spirit. One predominant characteristic of the Wilderness is the acquisition of silence, outwardly and inwardly.

You are not acquiring silence simply for its own sake. You are acquiring it as a means to fortify yourself on the journey of your soul. Silence is a communication device between you and yourself, and ultimately between you and God. In silence you are just *being*. The absence of doing enables you to get in touch with the real you. When you are in touch with your soul, your soul can get in touch with God—or the source, whichever name you prefer. When you are in touch with the source, you begin to have a relationship with it. Just knowing that something higher exists is the beginning. The more time you spend in silence and stillness, the more aware you become that something or someone else is with you, and that you are with something or someone else as well.

There will come a time when the foundation of spiritual laws learned in the Wilderness is firmly established in your consciousness, and Moses is no longer needed. When it is time for you to demonstrate the spiritual laws learned in the Wilderness, Joshua will take over the reigns of leadership in your consciousness. Your Joshua consciousness is the new thought system by which you will now live. It will govern you.

COMPASS

Once you give up your material identity, can you identify with a nonmaterial part of you that feels alive for the first time?

3

Beginning Your Dialogue

GOD SPEAKS. THAT IS RIGHT: the source of all creation has a voice, and he uses that voice. In the Wilderness you initiate your first direct contact with the source.

You do not hear a voice initially. Contact begins usually as a feeling of intuition, a slight pulse of energy leading in a particular direction. The energy is usually so slight that you can easily miss it if you are not careful. But if you become aware of it and follow it, you will be led somewhere that you are supposed to go. For me, it was usually to a book I should read. The color of the book, or its title, somehow appeared to me much brighter than the surrounding books in a bookstore. Or a title would stick in my head that I could not mentally shake, and I would see it over and over again.

Amazing things—which some might deem coincidences—started to occur. I would see different television shows featuring my name in a scenario I was currently undergoing in my real life. In spiritual circles we say that there is no such thing as coincidence—only God incidents. I was having many of them, so much so that I began to notice them everywhere. I started to see them as little miracles, such as when my car stalled and I prayed it into working. I would randomly open up some spiritual literature, after praying to be guided to the right words, and there they were. We all have these incidents. They seem quite ordinary to most of us. We take them for granted, without pausing to ponder the miraculous origins. I had time on my hands, so I did ponder them.

The biggest obstacle in communing with God, I found initially, is suspending disbelief that you can actually hear God's voice. It was an issue of worth. Who was I to be talking to God? To me, at this point, God was someone impersonal. God was not a personal relation in my life like, say, a friend I could talk to—or so I thought. If you can suspend your disbelief for long enough, an amazing and life-changing dialogue will occur between you and your Creator.

For me it started when I read the *Conversations with God* (CWG) book series by Neale Donald Walsch.[1] I was fortunate enough to correspond with the author for a period of time through an AOL website, before the book really took off. For anybody who has not read these amazing books, it is one of the must-read books series in existence. I started reflecting on some of the books' concepts after my daily reading sessions. I started asking questions, both aloud and inwardly, about what I had read. One day I was startled to hear responses to my questions in my mind. At first I did not pay too much attention. Then, gradually, I started asking follow-up questions to what I was hearing. A dialogue began. One day I asked whom I was talking to, and the voice in my head said, "I Am that I Am, my child."

That is the only name that the voice has ever given me. This is how we start all of our dialogues. I say, "Are you God?" and the voice says, "I Am that I Am."

It is not an easy process talking to God, but it is very doable. You must be in tune, almost like a radio frequency, to the signal from which God operates. In order to do this, you must clear your head of your own thoughts, and listen very carefully in silence. If you are still struggling with disbelief and denial of any kind about whom you are talking to, you will break the connection quickly.

I learned that suspension of disbelief is the first step in talking to God. After it was proven to my satisfaction that Neale Donald Walsch (or anyone else, for that matter) could talk to God, I asked myself why I could not do the same. The idea was introduced into my consciousness; it stuck and took root. I believe that, as a result of reading the first CWG book, I tapped into a frequency that allowed me to hear God's voice. Others may connect on other frequencies, but for me the God found in these books was the God I intuitively felt to be real.

Of course I had all the same doubts as anyone else. I asked myself how I knew that I was really talking to God and not myself—or possibly someone else. The only answer I can give, similar to the one that Walsch gave in CWG, is that one moment I asked God a question I did not know the answer to. Five seconds later, I did know.

God became my friend, one I could talk with about anything. Our friendship evolved from many conversations. Most of our conversations were of a personal nature, and involved questions that directly pertained to my life. It took about a year from those first encounters with God to get to the place where true dialogue with God began.

God talks in a strange way. His language and the energy surrounding it are always so filled with love. It did not matter what low emotional state I was coming from; the only energy I ever got back was love. To be honest, this sometimes annoyed me. Was not God capable of anger and frustration? If so, it was never shown to me. God used endearments like "dear heart," "little one," and always "my child" when talking to me. These were my clues that it really was God.

Sometimes I heard other words in my mind, words which I do not believe came from God. The energy was not of love, so it became important to identify clearly in my mind when it was indeed God. I would ask the Holy Spirit to connect me to the I Am, or God. At first I used to ask, "Are you the God of Abraham or the God of *Conversations with God*?" for identity purposes. Then I stopped needing as much reassurance. I still need quite a bit though—all of my dialogues with God start by me asking, "Are you God?"

I have found that the best time to interact with God is right after I awaken, after meditating, and on Saturday mornings. The connection to God seems the clearest at these times. It is much easier to hear God's voice then. God speaks and cares enough to listen and respond.

I can tell you from personal experience that the anger and blame we project towards God is accepted. No lightning bolts from heaven come for you—although I have looked up a couple of times to make sure. You quickly begin to understand that in a world where there is free will, it makes no sense to blame God for the state of the world. I decided that, because I could not blame God for the state of the world, I could blame God for giving us free will in the first place. But I knew that my argument was ridiculous. If God did not give us free will, we could not make any choices. We would be like robots. What would be the point of that?

In one of my first dialogues with God I asked, "Who are we really?"—meaning human beings, in relation to him. God told me that we are similar to him in the way that offspring are to their parents. We are part of him and one with him, but we still have an individual and separate identity. We are God's body. It is like we are cells in the whole body called God. Each cell has an individual blueprint, each is unique, but each cell is part of the whole body. A cell lives in relation to the other millions of cells inside of a body. Many cells may interact and be aware of the other cells. But how many are aware of the body as a whole, in its entirety? All the functions and abilities inherent to each cell are integral to that of the whole entity in which it lives.

Our soul's mission is to come to Earth and have experiences that we call forth. We do this in order for our soul to obtain a certain level of spiritual development. The experiences that we call forth are quite specific in nature, and directly relate to the areas most in need of healing inside of us. Much of the pain we feel from challenging experiences stems from the fact that we are unaware of what is being worked out in our subconscious during these times. On a conscious level, you are only aware of the pain or discomfort you feel. As a result, many people at this time do not stop to ask themselves why they are having these sets of experiences at all. When one is challenged on any level, the question to ask is: What are these challenges here to teach me?

Nobody enjoys pain, and the purpose of the soul on Earth is neither to learn about, nor to teach pain to others. Its purpose is to grow exponentially upwards. To the soul this is a very difficult assignment. Most souls return to Earth without any conscious knowledge of where they have been before. Their memories are blocked from knowingness. This creates anxiety in the mind of the individual on Earth. The mind then chooses of its own volition to separate from the spirit, and a chasm occurs where the soul no longer exists as the whole identity of an individual, but instead is relegated to the far reaches of one's consciousness.

The mind takes center stage and dominates for most of an unconscious individual's life. The mind creates a separate self with its own Earthly beliefs, desires, and imagined needs. This separate self creates an Earthly identity for itself. The mind is such a powerful creative tool that the identity it conceives for itself comes to believe that it is real.

Thus, the true dilemma begins. We are here on Earth quite purposefully, yet without any memory of the purpose for our existence. The soul knows, but the soul is no longer part of the conscious equation. The hole or space left by the soul's banishment to the back of our consciousness creates in human beings a longing: a longing for truth, meaning, and purpose in our lives. In order to fill that space left by our soul, the ego or new identity we have created for ourselves decides to seek fulfillment outside of itself. In the world outside, it goes on a mad hunt for things or people to appease its longings. The longer it takes to fulfill its demands, the longer the ego remains preoccupied and fails to realize the truth.

The quickest way for the ego to realize the truth is, first, to satisfy its desires. It is much more difficult when the desires of the ego have not been satisfied; this can delay spiritual growth indefinitely. The ego will cling to the illusion that the answer exists outside of itself, until there is evidence to prove it wrong. In other words, until you get what you think you want, you will not realize that what you have does not really satisfy you after all.

After successfully accomplishing the ego's agenda, human beings are then plagued with the question, "Now what?" What more can I do, be, or have in order to feel whole? This longing is the very thing that leads them to reconnect with the soul that was abandoned by the mind. In Egypt the soul asks them, "are you sure you really want the answer to the question, 'what now?'" If the individual is sufficiently weary with the present condition of their life, their answer will be yes. If they are not, they will remain in the land of Egypt until they are ready.

Some may never be ready to move any further than an Egypt consciousness in this lifetime, and that is all right. Every soul will develop in its own time. Individuals enter into the Wilderness to commune with their soul, and to reclaim it as a part of them. In the Wilderness, identifying with the human mind as representing who one is must voluntarily be surrendered. This is the only way one can identify with an awakened aspect of themselves—in other words, their soul.

The Wilderness is a challenging phase of development where people may linger for a long time. This is because it is not an easy process to give up one's old concept of self in order to discover one's real self. Old habits and ways of being die hard. The Wilderness is the place where they must be crucified. In the Wilderness, your human persona and identity are taken away quite literally, and you are left with nothing but your true self.

After the image of yourself—that image which you thought was real for so long—is gone, you will begin to become aware of your true self as something more. The seed of this new identity must germinate and develop in your consciousness until you become aware of it as the real you. The soul that was once imprisoned has now been set free. If you are conscious of what is going on spiritually, you will allow this process to unfold naturally.

If you are still unaware that what is going on your life has its basis in spirit, you will continue to resist this process. Your denial will bring about even more painful lessons, the purpose being to compel you to give up the identity your ego has created for itself. You must lay this false identity down. There is no other way. Herein lies the problem: how can you give up who you think you are? The answer is that you cannot. Then the definitive question becomes, "Who am I?" After you answer this question, you will learn that which is not real—the *false* identity you created—is what is being surrendered. In the Wilderness you give up the false self for your *authentic* self.

How do you plan to start talking and interacting consciously with God?

4

Discovering Your Soul

WHY DO MOST PEOPLE CHOOSE to create another self? There is no need for you to do so. Your real self is always available for you to access at any time. It is because you find it far easier to create externally than to go on an internal journey to discover the truth about your real identity. The world inside is not a stimulating one to many people; it lacks the sensory input found in the outer world. The world inside may seem scary, boring, or uninteresting.

Herein lies the dilemma. It bears repeating. You cannot get the mental stimulation that the world provides when you go inside. The inner world will not provide you mentally with what you think you need. The soul exists at a higher level than the mental one. The problem is that you think that you are your mind, because you so closely identify with it.

You believe your mind to *be* you, instead of it being *a part of* you. You also identify with the physical body, and believe it to be you as well. Why?

In order for the soul to come to Earth and gain the experiences that it seeks, it had to create a body, history and persona that would allow it to accomplish its goals on Earth. After the package was ready, the soul incarnated to Earth and the package was born. The package was not the soul, and the soul was not the package. They were two separate entities, sharing one experience. Although the package was created to house the soul, it took on a life of its own after its birth. It was born into a particular family, had particular friends, lived in a particular part of the world, and looked a particular way. All of these particulars occupied the mind of the package for so long that it never took the time to look and see what it carried inside.

The package has another name. It can also be called the human personality.

Why did the soul not nudge the package and make it aware of its existence? To do so would violate the agreement that the soul made to come here. Its purpose was to learn from the experiences of the package. The soul learned in silence. When the package became curious about the soul's existence and sought it out, the soul would make contact.

This agreement was made before coming to Earth, and thus the soul waited in silence. The soul observed the life experiences of the package, and influenced it subtly by sending it higher energy. It did so silently, hoping to influence the package to seek out the highest outcomes possible. If the package had ever taken the time to trace the source of its intuitive guidance, it would have been made aware of the soul earlier.

The stage is set for the soul's arrival into conscious awareness of the package when it begins to ask the question, "What now in life?" The soul answers, "*I* am now!"

My goal in the Wilderness stage of development was to try and find my calling in life. I read the appropriate books on the subject and studied all of the appropriate literature available. Advice ranged from your calling being what interested you most as a child, to being the thing you are naturally good at. No answer really seemed to apply directly to me; I still felt lost. After a while I stopped caring about what I was to do, as long as it was something that God wanted me to do.

I remember my prayer. "Dear God," I said, "please use me in your service. I do not care in what area, because nothing in particular interests me. I can sweep the streets or become a nun, or become a missionary in Africa. But please use me, your child." And then I said my name.

There were songs that I learned from a songbook, when I went on a spiritual retreat to my church headquarters, which I sang during this time. One song that resonated deeply within me was called "Here I am, Lord."[1] I mention this song because the chorus made me think for the first time: maybe God had need of *us*, instead of us always needing God.

During the Wilderness experience I gave up all of my attachments to worldly things. I attempted to empty myself of ego as much as possible, and was now ready to be of service to God in some way. I prayed and searched diligently for guidance on what I was supposed to do in life.

The first clue I received came while reading the second book of the *Conversations with God* series. Before picking up any spiritual literature, I had the habit of praying to God to automatically lead me to the right page. Sometimes I did not think that he heard me, because I was sure that some of the pages that I turned to could not really apply to me. Or maybe it was because I was not willing to accept what was said on those pages.

But on this one particular day, on my first attempt after opening up the book, I landed on page 122. The author was talking about the need to reform the educational system, and the need for an effective and different model based on spiritual principles. I thought to myself, "Are you telling me to teach, Lord?"

I had thought about teaching before, briefly. I had rejected the idea because, although I liked the idea of teaching, I was not all that keen on teaching facts. I liked the idea of having summers off, and not working in an office. However, I was not sure that I had the patience necessary to work with children. In fact, I was sure that I did not. I was not even sure how I felt about being around children all day. I used to refer to them affectionately as the cartoon characters "Rugrats." I used to babysit infants when I was younger. I loved babies; it was when they turned into little children that I began to have my doubts.

I was listening to a Christian radio station one day, and heard an advertisement for a Montessori school in the city where I was living. I thought that the word Montessori was strange. I had never heard it before, but it stuck in my head. A couple of weeks later, I was looking through the local city newspaper in the job listings section, and I came upon a tiny ad for an aide at a Montessori private school just seven minutes from my house. I thought, "there goes that name again." All the while I was questioning God, saying, "Is this what you want for me to do?" I decided to call the school. I was asked to go in for an interview. All I kept thinking was that I had never worked with children before.

I went to the interview, and was told I was overqualified to be an aide. Regardless, I let them know that I was interested in the position. I started working the next day for about seven dollars an hour. I could not believe that after a couple of years of being still, I was actually working. At first it was just the afternoon nap shift, and then the aftercare program. But after about a month, I was working as a full-time aide in one of the upper elementary classrooms.

I loved the job. What I loved most was that every day was creative. No two days were ever the same; you could choose how you wanted to create and spend each day. There was so much room for creative expression and freedom. Children worked on the floor, on rugs or outside in the grass. There was no rigid structure or routine, which I loved. This was a breath of fresh air after years of working in an office.

After working as an aide for about six months, I decided I wanted to become a Montessori teacher. The problem was that, in order to be the type of teacher I wanted to be, I had to go to graduate school and get a Masters Degree in Montessori education. But I had no money. Although I loved my job, being an aide barely gave me enough money to survive on financially.

I was certain this was what God wanted me to do at this time in my life. I was fortunate that of the few international Montessori training facilities in the world, one was on the outskirts of Baltimore, Maryland, at the time that I attended, about an hour and a half away from me. School ended in June, and the Masters program I had found was to start in July. So I sent in an application to graduate school, even though I could barely scrape up the application fee, and anxiously awaited the reply.

I was accepted into the program. But in order to hold my spot they needed $500, which I did not have, so I did not send it in.

The Sunday night before school was to start, I still had no news about the student loan that I applied for. I did not know what to do—school was starting the next day. But I heard a voice in my head say clearly when I was praying, I was to take my black book bag out of the closet and to go to school on Monday.

To say I was petrified was an understatement. I was being asked to drive, soon after having a second car accident, for more than an hour on the treacherous Baltimore 695 Beltway. I had only had my car back for a week. To me, Baltimore's 695 lanes are reminiscent of the Indianapolis 500 Speedway. To say I did not like lanes that curve is the understatement of the year. I remembered later a fellow student telling me how much she enjoyed driving on 695. I guess it was a matter of perspective. I had little choice in the matter; spirit was beckoning.

I wept most of Sunday night out of sheer fright. I did not know which scared me the most: the drive to school, or the lack of money. My aunt had bought me a cell phone in case of an emergency. My cousin gave me $20 for gas money that night. On Monday, I left the house about six a.m. to find my way to school. I got a little lost, but I made it there in one piece. I went into the classroom and, much to my surprise, they had a nametag with my name on it. Maybe, I thought, I was supposed to be here after all.

There was only one problem. I had not paid for the preparatory class, and I still did not know if the student loan I had applied for would come through in time. I sat in the hallway during breaks and prayed to the Lord, beseeching him to allow me to stay. I felt like a phony, like I did not belong. My mind could not accept what I was doing, but I was stepping out on faith anyway. I had come too far in the Wilderness to start doubting God now. I was sure that this was where he had led me.

I attended school on faith for one week, until school administrators came to class and said that those who owed money would have to pay by Friday. I was sure that they were talking to me. On Friday, I went to talk to the financial aid people to tell them that my student loan check had not come yet, and I was unsure of my status. Much to my dismay, I was told that we were supposed to pay for the preparatory class out of pocket, and that the student loan check would only take care of the school year starting in September.

I was flabbergasted. In my world, no one I knew—including me—could pay $2000 out of pocket. I was in an international program with people from Canada, one from Haiti; the rest were mostly from out of state. I could not believe that they could afford to pay that amount of money out of pocket for the course.

The jig was up: there was no way I could stay. I did my week of faith, and I was out of gas money, much less anything else. I told God that I was not going back to school on Monday. Although I was being led by blind faith, I said I would not take a step further, not without his direct intervention. If this was what he told me to do, he would have to make a way. I spent the weekend praying and mentally fasting with God, begging him to find a way for me to continue doing something that I really wanted to do.

At 8:31 a.m. on Monday morning, one minute after class was supposed to start, I realized that this was it. Things were not going to work out. My mind could not absorb the shock. I really felt I had been led every step of the way. Had I gone wrong somewhere, missed a sign or signal? I could not imagine the life I would have if things did not work out. I could not imagine going back to the unfulfilling life I had, with no purpose from spirit. There was nothing I could do. I told God that if this were his will, I would find a way to bear it. In that moment I surrendered and gave up the fight.

One minute later, the phone rang. It was the head instructor telling me to come to school; she did not want me to miss any instruction time. She said that we would work something out. My miracle had come. My girlfriend left home to bring me gas money so that I could drive to school. I am a strong believer in miracles—I am a first-hand product of them.

I went to school, and it took about three weeks for everything to get sorted out. I had to meet with numerous people about my "special circumstances" several times. They told me they had not even received my $500 deposit. I felt like a charity case, but that was just my pride—at least I got to stay. I remember my instructor telling me that I changed the program in my first week: because of me, she said, people could now pay for the summer class when their student loan check came in the fall.

I was the first exception to the rule. I did not ask God to be the first exception, nor did I particularly want to be, but there you have it. Is there not some saying that when God calls you, he pays your way? I have done some challenging things in my life to date, but that program was one of the most challenging.

COMPASS

34

Can you recall a miracle that occurred in your life?

5

Creation Becomes the Purpose

IF MIRACLES ARE ELEVATED TO the status of the impossible or the rarely occurring, then what good are they? Miracles are everyday occurrences, according to *A Course in Miracles*. I believe it. When you are aligned closely with God, miracles become very natural. Being in the Wilderness lets you elevate your consciousness until you are so in tune with the divine, and the divine is so in tune with you, that miracles often result. I call this process "reaching Mt. Zion." You work on your consciousness until it reaches the summit of spiritual knowingness. Then you can commune in love and faith with God in consciousness.

What is a miracle? A miracle is when you allow the possibility to exist, first in your consciousness, about an outcome you desire. Then you refuse to believe in any possibility occurring other than the one you desire. You do this even when you are bombarded by factual illusions to the contrary. Imagine Daniel in the lion's den. By refusing to allow into your consciousness anything but the truth of divine law that states that your thoughts create your reality—and by holding steadfastly to this truth—you bring about miracles.

The truth of divine law is that everything is creative; thus you create what you desire to occur. Accepting other people's versions of reality does not serve you or anybody else. If your belief in the power of God is strong enough, it will move mountains in your life. This process is undertaken by first mentally removing any obstacles that block good from being expressed in physical form in your life. Everything in the world is made out of energy, including your thoughts. All thoughts are creative, so in order to produce miracles you must hold a creative thought in the energy of love, and have faith in its outcome. You do this by having a close union with God—a partnership in fact. Your thoughts are partnered with and connected to the energy of the Universe: God energy. The end result is a miracle.

What is God energy? It is the energy that surrounds everything that has substance, basically all that exists. We are made up of that energy too. We are created in the image and likeness of God, so the same energy that exists in God and the Universe exists in us. Tapping into the same energy that lives inside of us, and that lives inside of God, is what produces miracles.

Energy, when expressed on Earth, solidifies into some form. The form the energy takes depends on how the energy is shaped by creative substance. Neutral creative substance is found in us, in the form of thoughts. God brought the physical world into being, by using his creative ability to form the physical Earth through the energy of thought. Whether the thought manifested into physical reality in six days or 4.54 billion years is not important.

What *is* important is that we too have this power to create. We create by taking the energy we are made up of—love—and then imagining into substance what we desire to manifest: the people, things, or events in our lives. Love is the energy that surrounds everything, and it is the most creative force of all.

Few of us use this gift of creative power productively in our lives. The reason is simple: we do not really believe we have the power to create anything in our lives. If we did, why would our lives be in such a state? Why indeed? Could it be because, in the absence of using our creative power consciously, we allowed life and circumstances to create *us*? We became a product of our life's circumstances, instead of life becoming a product of our creative ability. If the real you—spirit—does not create your life the way you want it, then your life will be created in the image of your ego. This is the way it works.

We must use the power that God has placed in each of us to create what we desire to manifest. Not using your power is a decision. It is a decision to be a victim of your life circumstances and blame God for the condition of your life. Did Christ not say that we too are Gods? He said this because it is true. The process by which God creates is the same process that is accessible to us, to use in any way we choose.

All life is creative. In order to stop being a victim to circumstances in our lives, we must learn how to use creativity in the way it was intended. The question then becomes: How do we use this creative force?

We do so by acknowledging the bitter—or liberating—truth, whichever way you see it. The truth is that we create what occurs in our own lives. Is that not a thought that fills you with dread? For most of us, we have not created our lives the way they are, at least not consciously. We have instead allowed life to create through us by default. By not taking an active role in creating our lives, we settled for what showed up.

Do you see the error? By not consciously and consistently using our God-given power of creativity, the end result is our life being the way it is. But it is a life that we did not actively participate in creating. If you love the life that you have, great—these words are not for you. But those of you who are unhappy with the state of the affairs in your lives: I am talking to you.

Life was never meant to be non-creative. It was meant to be a creative endeavor, with power given to you to create whatever you choose. This provides you with the opportunity to express yourself as God on Earth.

For many, this chore has been too much. The ability to create has lain dormant in people for so long. This is a travesty. All that you want to have and to create awaits you. But you must choose to create it consciously, or it will be created for you by default.

How do you create consciously? Decide what you really want for your life. Then decide that you will accept nothing less. After you hold this vision in consciousness, nothing less can come to you—the present state of your consciousness will not accept anything less. The very energy of anything less cannot shape itself into any solid form, because you are vibrating at a higher frequency than the lower-level energy at which you settle. God's children do not settle. We do not accept anything less than what we can imagine.

The problem is that many of us do not envision a great deal. We settle for less on a regular basis. Why? It is an issue of worthiness, and not knowing who we truly are. If we knew we were created with the same divine substance as God, and it is our birthright to use the same creative force that God used to create the Earth, would we act differently? I think so.

So the first step in using the creative power of God is to recognize that you have it inside of you. The second step is to imagine what the highest vision of your life looks like. The third step is to use the creative force of God to bring this vision into fruition. The fourth step is to refuse to settle for anything less than the highest vision that you can imagine. If you choose to settle, you do not really believe step one—so you must return to it until you can accept this truth. Then you can proceed with the rest of the steps.

You do not have to create alone; God longs to create with you. In fact, God will guide you on what you should seek to create. It is not because God has a preference about what you should create, but because he knows the very thing you hold in your heart of hearts—your secret desires. These desires are the very ones you have buried deep within you and are afraid to examine.

We do not claim our secret desires because we feel unworthy of receiving them. We have spent so much time in the world giving up our so-called selfish nature, learning false humility, that we feel guilty knowing we have greatness inside of us. We feel this way even though we know that the Almighty created us with greatness and splendor inside of us. What are we guilty of? Hiding our own talents and refusing to claim them until they disappear from lack of use is the legacy of shame we have inherited.

We must get to a place where we learn to put our *real* self first—our spiritual self. We can never go wrong when we come from a true place of spirit inside of us. We might misinterpret what we think spirit is saying, but if we are certain we cannot go wrong. You cannot hurt anybody else by being successful, and by using your creative talents given to you by God. The very fear that keeps so many of us from using our creative power is strangling the life right out it.

Our biggest fear is that we cannot do whatever it is that we desire to do. You are right: you cannot do it, and you are not being asked to. Your part in the equation is to empty yourself of you. Then you must allow your spirit to serve as a conduit for divine inspiration to flow through, in whichever way it chooses. It is not you doing the work; spirit is working through you. This should alleviate much of your fear.

The next common fear can be summed up by the prayer, "Why me, Lord?" "Why *not* me?" is the question that you should ask yourself. What is wrong with you? The answer is: nothing. God knows this, which is why he placed talent within you. Is God wrong about you, or are you wrong about yourself? If you do not have a high enough opinion about yourself, accept God's opinion of you. Believe in it until you can authentically come to the same place of esteem about yourself that God holds.

God longs to create through you. Allow him to—move yourself out of the way. The more you tap into the creative power *inside* yourself, the more you will create *outside* yourself. Discipline is required in creating. You must discipline yourself to create a little each day, even when you are filled with fear. The more you walk through your fears by creating despite them, the faster they will go away. It is amazing that we so often fear the things that are best for us. Why is it that we do not fear the things that limit us?

If you walk closely with God, he will do the work for you. But he must have an open vessel through which to express. It is not even necessary that you believe in the end result ahead of time. Before you reach the end, or when you reach it, the vision will become real to you. As it has been said, sometimes you must "fake it until you make it." Use your life to do something creative.

COMPASS

How can you be of service to humanity?

6

Crossing the Jordan River

YOUR MOSES CONSCIOUSNESS HAS GONE as far as it can go. When you begin to identify with a higher aspect of yourself as the real you, it is time for you to leave the Wilderness stage of spiritual development. Moses has led his people (the limiting thoughts in your head) through the Wilderness for a substantial period of time. Joshua, who emerges as the predominant ruler in your consciousness, now takes over; he will lead the thought people in your head through the Jordan River and into the Promised Land.

According to *The Metaphysical Bible Dictionary*, "There is a stream of thought constantly flowing through the subconsciousness, made up of thoughts good, bad and indifferent, which is typified in Scripture by the river Jordan." In the words of Charles Fillmore, "This thought stream has to be crossed before the Children of Israel can go over into the Promised Land."[1]

What is the Jordan River stage of spiritual development? "The Jordan can also be said to represent that place in consciousness where we are willing to meet the results of our thoughts, face to face."[2] It is the stage in which you must overcome internally the adverse and fear-filled thoughts that limit your spiritual progress. This is done by surmounting obstacles, which appear as unmovable mountains in your life. Your thoughts and belief systems, steeped in pessimism, must be challenged and defeated.

The Jordan River gives you an opportunity to defeat adverse thoughts that are blocking your good from manifesting on Earth. Consistently holding adverse thoughts in your mind is the very thing that draws obstacles to you in the physical world. A belief in anything being greater than God is the primary adverse thought you must overcome.

The purpose of the Jordan River is to bring our shadowy fears (thoughts that dwell in your subconscious) to the light of truth found in conscious awareness. This occurs in order for us to defeat those fears by denying their ability to affect us adversely in any way. We must elevate our limiting thoughts into higher conscious awareness, where our only belief is in the power and presence of God. Our evolved belief system liberates our consciousness from a mental enslavement to fear.

The degree to which troubling adverse thoughts or waters afflict your consciousness is significant; it will determine how long you will remain inside the banks of the Jordan River. You must calm these troubled waters or thoughts, and pass through them, in order to enter the Promised Land. You usually stay in the Jordan River phase for about 12 to 18 months during your first foray into the journey of the soul.

Our Joshua consciousness will lead us into the Promised Land. Joshua is born in us when we transcend fearful thoughts that seek to prevent us from taking action. "The only difference between Joshua and Jesus is the extent of conscious realization of identity with the I Am. When we know the law of spiritual demonstration and have the courage to act, we are Joshua."[3] Our fears cause us to give our power over to the false gods that we make of lack and limitation. We then worship these false gods by becoming enslaved in consciousness to them when we let them control us. When we can bring our thoughts under the command of spiritual law that recognizes the power of God as our only reality, we reach a new, higher stage of spiritual development called the Promised Land.

The Jordan River phase of spiritual development is not an easy one; it is one of the most challenging stages to progress through. On a daily basis, you are called upon to challenge the inner fears that plague you. During the Jordan River stage, you literally shake with fear with every step you take to overcome the challenges that arise. But fear will not prevent you from being able to move forward, because you will realize that you have come too far to turn back now: the only option is to continue forward. You must find a way to move through the energy of fear and do the work necessary to overcome it, no matter how difficult.

When I was in the Jordan River in the life area of work, I often wept from sheer fright. I was called forth to challenge some of my biggest fears in life. The seeming enormity of the challenges overwhelmed me. After the first car accident I mentioned previously, I had another one—this time with my new car. I am certain that repeated car accidents, over a relatively short span of time, are spirit's way of getting your attention. (It also can be that I was not a good driver.) Whenever people tell me that they had numerous car accidents in a short period of time, I always ask them, "what did they teach you?"

Spirit attempts to show us what we hold in our subconscious mind—in my case, fear and anger. I had too many serious car accidents in a short timeframe to see them just as coincidences. The Universe was trying to get my attention and show me something. It worked. As a result of having these accidents, I became conscious of my role in causing them. The outer consequences (my car accidents) resulted from the fear I was succumbing to in my mind. The Universe was forcing to me to face these fears head-on, so to speak.

In the Jordan River stage, you have to take one day at a time. Each day is filled with sufficient challenges. The process and the journey—not the destination—are what become important when you are in the Jordan. The destination becomes a mere byproduct of the journey; you attain it seemingly quickly when you are no longer focused on reaching it. The real learning and value take place on the roads you travel to reach the destination.

The Jordan River is a stage where you work towards the manifestation of something. The more you accustom yourself to owning your aspirations, the easier and less overwhelming it will be when your dreams manifest. If you already had the consciousness necessary for manifesting your desires, there would be no delay in the manifestation of those desires. There would be no Jordan River stage of development, so to speak. But most people are not at this level of consciousness, so the Jordan River is a necessary stage. This stage enables you to accept the good that is yours, in consciousness, so that when your desires manifest, you can peacefully and lovingly accept them.

Time is not your enemy, though to most people it seems that way. Why is that? They see time as something that prevents them from experiencing their desires in the here and now. The truth of the matter is: time is your friend. It gives you the opportunity to establish, first in consciousness, the conditions necessary for your desires to manifest in your life. In order to do this, you must develop a place of receptivity in your consciousness for the things you desire to show up. If you do not first lay a foundation of receptivity, manifestations will be delayed.

Our time in the Jordan provides an excellent opportunity to use time as it was intended: to help produce miracles. The initial purpose of time was as a frame of reference to use in the creation process. In the absence of now, there had to be an alternative. So time was created as a useful tool for referencing a place other than now. The question we ask on Earth is, "If not now, then when?" "Time" is the answer to that question. In the world of spirit there is only now. Thus there is no need for time as we know it. We are able to create, instantly.

Things are different on Earth. You are not able to access the full capabilities of your spirit, so you need a "when." The notion of "when" becomes indicative of some time in the future. Time is a tool created to help you on Earth when you cannot create instantaneously in the now. Time is neither the problem nor the enemy. It is a tool and a gift, given to you by spirit so that you can help yourself. If you are not using the tool correctly, why blame the tool? Why assign blame at all? Is it not better to learn the correct way of using the tool—the way it was intended?

Time gives you the illusion that something other than now exists. In truth, we know in spirit that now is all that exists, so something other than now cannot really exist. "Now" is absolute in spirit. On Earth, "now" is relative to something else—you fill in the blanks: "when I am ready," "when I feel worthy," "tomorrow," and so on.

Time is one indication of your conscious ability to produce. If you want to know the level of your consciousness, observe how quickly what you desire manifests. This may seem harsh: you could argue that there are many valid reasons why time is necessary in the process of manifestation. If your consciousness were at a high enough level of vibration, whatever you desired would manifest instantly. Jesus, the Christ, was able to do this—and so can you. The problem lies in thinking you need time to develop the necessary level of consciousness, in doubting that you already have it.

To develop a high degree of consciousness is not to work on it slowly until you feel you have enough. The highest level of spiritual awareness is to accept, and to know already, that you always have the amount of energy needed to manifest anything. If you remember who you are—knowing that you are made up of spirit, divine substance, and absolute truth—then connecting with all the creative forces within enables you to manifest your desires on Earth instantly.

There is much more than you are aware of at your present level of consciousness. The spiritual gifts or abilities you have received from God are real as well. Use your divine gifts bequeathed to you from God, and know that you have the power to instantly manifest whatever you desire.

A delay in receiving your manifestations, and an ill use of time, suggest that you do not know the truth. You use time as a way to mentally accept your dreams one small piece at a time, until you feel comfortable in accepting them as a whole. This is a slow process. Time serves here as a slowing-down force of energy. Why not use it as an immediate force of energy? Know the truth about yourself now. You have the power to create all that you desire in an instant—this power was given to you by the I Am. So if you are not creating instantaneously, ask yourself why.

We may blame God for the time it takes for our desires to manifest. Why blame God? God gave us time as a tool to help us in creation. Why are we using this tool improperly? Maybe we do not know how to use it. Perhaps further explanation is needed.

When there is something you desire, know that it is yours. It became yours at the instant you desired it. Did Christ not teach this? Instead you doubt, question, consider your worthiness, and look at outer conditions for evidence of manifestation first, before you believe. You use time as a delaying mechanism when you refuse to accept the truth that you have what you desire at the moment you desire it. If you could just accept this truth, at the moment of desire—without any doubt or need for external evidence—you would create instantaneously. Thus time would be used properly, as a tool of manifesting in the now, and (as in the realm of spirit) now would be all that existed.

All thought is creative, so as soon as you create a thought surrounded by the divine substance of love, it is created instantly. If it does not instantly manifest, you have not acquired a high enough level of spiritual vibration to attract your desires to you. You are too filled with your own stuff. Spirit is awaiting an empty space within you that it can fill with truth.

What you call miracles on Earth are everyday natural occurrences in spirit. The mind is intended as a creative tool to imagine your desires and help manifest those desires. Instead, your mind is filled with all sorts of stuff that make it almost impossible for your dreams to manifest in a reasonable timeframe. The only reasonable timeframe is now, but on Earth this is not the case. You need to find a solution to the problem. The solution is easy, but challenging to implement. Clear your mind of unnecessary thoughts—which in most cases is almost all of them.

Think about all of the negative thoughts you have on a daily basis; then think about the creative energy of fear you used to surround these negative thoughts. Are you surprised when these thoughts manifest? They do not manifest instantly either. Much like your dreams, they take time to manifest. Why does it seem that the positive things you desire take so much longer than the negative to manifest? It is because you believe in the negative more than you believe in the positive. What you believe in is directly related to what does—or does not—manifest.

When manifestations occur that you deem negative, you blame God. Can you not see that the cause is the negative thoughts you held with an appropriate amount of fear? Usually you do not make this connection because of the delay between your first fearful thoughts and the undesirable outcome that results from holding those thoughts over a period of time. Fortunately for you, not all negative thoughts are manifested—can you imagine what would happen if they were? However, negative thoughts that are deeply felt with a high degree of fear (which is energizing) will manifest in some form or another when held over a long period of time.

You are a creative being. If you wish to continue creating the life you have, leave your mind in its current condition. If you desire a higher outcome, think higher thoughts. When negative thoughts enter your mind, you do not have to feed them with the energy of fear—do not feed them at all. Pay those thoughts no mind and they will fade into the background. When higher thoughts enter your mind, feed them with the energy of love. They will manifest if you have sufficient faith in God.

COMPASS

How can you be of service to humanity?

7

Stepping Stones in the Jordan

YOUR BELIEFS ARE WHAT LIMIT you from manifesting in an instant. How does one acquire a sufficient level of belief? The first belief that limits you is that you cannot create in an instant. This is an issue of worth and not knowing who you are; you must work on this. Another limiting belief is that God may deny your request. If your request is surrounded with the energy of love, why would God deny it? Are your requests surrounded by the energy of fear denied? No, they too manifest. So would not the higher ones manifest also?

God does not say "no" some of the time and "yes" at others; God always says "yes." That is why you have the power to manifest at all. If some of your desires could be denied, then why give you the power to create in the first place? That makes no sense. Are you suggesting that

God did not have any sense when endowing you with the ability to create? Or is it your beliefs that make no sense? If you want to make any significant and lasting spiritual progress, you must challenge the beliefs that limit you.

Another prevalent limiting belief is that you lack the power, conditions, or circumstances in the present moment to manifest your desires. Can you see that your present circumstances and conditions were created by your old beliefs? If so, how can you deny that they can be changed in an instant by the act of acquiring new beliefs? You cannot.

The truth is, change is scary—even if it is change for the higher and better. If change occurs too suddenly, it seems overwhelming. You use time as a way to temper these reactions. If you have time to accept mentally that what you desire is possible, you have an easier time accepting it. Who is really afraid? It is your mind. Instant manifestation threatens it. So the mind cunningly rejects instant manifestation, elevating it to the level of the impossible. The mental delay in accepting that you can have what you desire is detrimental to that desire ever manifesting.

Manifestation comes from spirit. It is not up to the mind to have a reaction; you must shut it down. Shut the mind down by emptying it of all thoughts and embracing your spirit. Your spirit will speak in feelings, or a sensation of energy bringing about peace, love, and joy. This is your spirit's reaction to the manifestation of your desires. Identify with this energy and its vibration; let go of anything contrary to it. The more you identify with your spirit, the less power the mind will have over you. It will become easier for you to create.

The highest way to effectively use spirit for the purpose of manifestation is to be attuned in consciousness, ahead of time, to an overall feeling of knowingness about a positive outcome. We are certain of many things, but we are not certain about good being the only reality. We usually have a general feeling of foreboding about our desires. We must tune our minds into the frequency of the divine. This enables us to enter into the energy of peace, health, and prosperity. When we are in this state, our consciousness becomes a stream of pure being, flowing in the energy of love.

A state of knowingness is all that is required to enter into this state. True knowingness stems from accessing a place of spirit within us. We know there is nothing we must do externally to receive our good, and nothing we must do to maintain it after we have received it. There is simply someone to be and to continuously be: our true and authentic spiritual self.

For many, accepting one's good is a hard thing. You experience an initial feeling of shock and surprise when your highest good is manifested. Although you have become comfortable with the idea of experiencing your dream in theory, it can feel overwhelming when that same dream manifests in the physical realm. How odd is it that, at the time you should be most joyful, when your conscious labors have brought about an abundant harvest, you are bombarded with feelings of unworthiness? What are you unworthy of? Love and greatness have always been yours, but you have not been ready for them to show up. How long will you continue to punish yourself with feelings of unworthiness?

Those who manifest abundantly on Earth accept their worthiness; it is time you do the same. You accept your worthiness by knowing that you are worthy. It is that simple. God is saying that you are worthy—why would you question God? What part of your self cannot accept this truth? It is your inauthentic ego.

The spirit is the part of you that you are still unsure of at this stage of your development. Your soul oscillates between two places of being: one of spirit and one of ego. This constant back-and-forth does not elicit confidence. In fact, it does the opposite: it erodes your confidence in who you really are. This back-and-forth must stop.

You must make a final choice, and refuse to accept any other false identity in consciousness. You are your spirit—you must not let yourself identify with any other versions of yourself. If you accept this truth deep within you, your struggle over identity will be over. Do not just think your way to this truth; know it in spirit. Tell yourself, "there is only one real me here—the other one is a 'false image that only *appears* to be real.'" The following affirmation may help:

I accept the truth about my true spiritual identity.

I lay claim to it.

I am a child of God, inherent and endowed

with the same abilities as my heavenly Father.

I will doubt no more.

I have always wondered about the difference between the words "soul" and "spirit." I have come to see spirit as the pure part of you that is connected to the source of all being, in a state of oneness. *Spirit* has no direct connection to your human personality. It is in union with the divine, and lives separately and apart from your human state of existence. You can tap into your spirit, but your spirit cannot tap into your human personality, because they live on two separate planes of existence. Think of your spirit as the divine part of yourself.

Your *soul*, while connected to your spirit, is at the same time aware of the part of you that is having a human experience. Your soul is the bridge that connects you on both sides: to your spirit on one side, and your human personality on the other. Through the bridge of your soul you can oscillate back and forth between each expression of your self.

If you are spirit, the questions become, "What is my body?," "What are my thoughts?," and "What is my human personality?" We will answer all of these questions.

What plagues humans most is concern about their bodies. You are not your body: you are made up of an infinite amount of energy substance, and only a partial amount is available to you on Earth. Your body is the container that enables you to live on Earth. In the truest sense of the word, a container is a thing that holds something else inside it. Your body does not hold your soul inside it, as many people believe—it is actually the other way around. However, a container is still a good visual you can identify with.

The body is actually created from a part of the energy coming from your spirit. It is contained in a field consisting of a sphere of light. Thus, the physical body can be thought of as made up of particles of light. But for our purposes, let us look at the body as a container of sorts. The body serves as a container of energy that enables us to live on Earth's frequency level. The actual design of this container was decided before we came here, its conditions carefully selected to allow us maximum growth potential. We despair of its size, color, height, and lack of—or too much of—certain individual features. Why is it that we do so?

The answer is simple. We do not really believe that we are spirit. We have bought into identifying with the body as who we really are on Earth. We did not choose to identify with our thoughts or even our hearts as who we are. We chose the body, and it has been the cause of so much grief for us ever since. The reason we chose the body is apparent, literally: it is the thing that we can see. It does not require a higher level of consciousness to relate to; it requires only our sense of sight. It was the easy choice. So the body became our identity and, as a result, our image of beauty. When we see our body as who we really are, the container becomes confused with the contained.

This error in thinking has caused us to level much hate and disgust at our container. The biggest judgment we level towards it is that we are not enough in the state we are in. It is good news that we are not the container—so the judgments we direct towards our bodies have no bearing on how we feel about our true selves. What sense does it make to hate a container, or to be unhappy with it? We could not do so if we did not identify the container as who we are. We are not the container; we are spirit. The container is merely a holder.

If you do not take care of something, it will not last very long. So the container should be cared for; that is common sense. If you care for your body, it will care for you and allow your spirit to remain on Earth longer. Be grateful to it for the true function it provides, for without it you could not live on Earth. It may be hard for you to accept the truth about your body, because you still identify with it as yourself. Let me ask you this: do you believe you will exist after your body is no longer alive? If your answer is yes, then how can you be your body? If your answer is no, ask yourself, would God create life to exist for only such a short period of time?

The work you have been doing entails a series of steps, like stepping stones leading you through the Jordan River and eventually to the shores of the Promised Land. Your time spent in the Jordan will consist of seemingly never-ending challenges. However, the Jordan River experience will come to an end, and it will be time to enter the Promised Land.

When you have mastered your fears and they no longer control your actions, you leave the Jordan River stage of spiritual development. Once you have learned how to combat your adversarial thoughts without allowing them to overcome you, you are ready to move to higher ground in consciousness. The Jordan River is a stage you are in when you are heading towards the "promise" that is yet to come.

When you enter the Promised Land it is now time for God's promise of good, or the highest desires of your heart, to manifest in your physical reality. Your higher consciousness has now been strengthened through trials in the Jordan River. Your consciousness is now ready to accept greatness, a prerequisite for the Promised Land.

When is it time to leave the Jordan River? You will be ready when you realize that "Miracles are natural. When they do not occur something has gone wrong."[1] as taught in *A Course in Miracles*. Also, when in the Jordan River your focus is no longer on when you will exit this stage of development. When you start to live in and accept the now as your only reality, you will be ready to leave the Jordan, and ready to enter into the Promised Land stage of spiritual development.

You will be led out of the Jordan River through a series of divine inspirations. They will appear as coincidences that you must recognize and follow through on. The divine guidance you receive will help to navigate your life, like a compass showing you the way. By following these directions, you will be led to your right and proper place. You will no longer have much fear and uncertainty about your future; you will have earned a greater appreciation for your spirit and its capabilities after leaving the Jordan River. Your Joshua consciousness, which has led you safely out of the Wilderness and through the Jordan River, is now ready to take you into the Promised Land.

How will you feel after your fears have actualized into physical reality?

8

Entering Canaan

YOU HAVE FINALLY ARRIVED! WHEN you first enter the Promised Land, you are confident in your future. The God that provided you with sustenance in the Wilderness, and helped you cross through the Jordan River, has now delivered you to a promised place. This place, the Promised Land, is also known as Canaan. "We also think of Canaan as referring to the sub-consciousness. Metaphysically it represents humbleness and receptivity. The land of Canaan, too, represents the unlimited elemental forces of Being in which man is placed, and to which he gives character through faith in God as omnipresent Spirit."[1]

When I first entered into Canaan, I was called to be a Montessori teacher at a public school in the inner city. I felt very humbled and grateful to be working in this new land. I was living out the manifestation of my dream to be of service. My entry into this new land was not as harmonious and welcoming as I would have liked, but I always felt safe and protected since I was aware of God's constant presence in my life. I knew I could not be driven from this Promised Land to which God had brought me—only on God's terms could I leave. In essence, I knew nobody could threaten my place in this new land. My true employer was God.

This did not mean that I was not challenged on a regular basis. I was new to the profession and still in a state of wonder over all that had occurred to bring me here. I was not yet fully grounded in my new role as a teacher, so I was a bit unsure how to proceed initially. I was in a new land, and I had worked so hard in the Jordan River to get here. It took me some time to accept that I was really here.

I have learned in life that when you are unsure of yourself, or humble, others may use this to indict you. They perceive humility, or displaying a lack of ego energy, as being incompetent. How ridiculous. People who constantly brag about their so-called abilities are the ones that I would question. If you are endowed with some gift or ability, you do not have to work so hard for people to acknowledge it. Recognition will come naturally, with time and hard work, when you come from a place of spirit instead of ego.

I was faced with confrontations immediately in my work environment. This is not surprising to me in hindsight, considering that I was entering new territory. But at the time, I was shocked. I thought to myself, "This cannot be the Promised Land!" The events I was experiencing occurred as the result of internal doubts still lingering in my consciousness; I had yet to deal with those doubts. In Montessori there is the erroneous belief that its practitioners should display perfection in every way. I saw people striving for outward perfection—but in my opinion, these very same people did not seem concerned about inner perfection.

On the whole, my experiences—particularly with the children—were positive. In truth, my spirit was unaffected by my negative teaching experiences. I chose to focus on *why* these experiences were occurring. I decided to look at what was occurring as lessons for growth, arising in the outer world as an opportunity for healing. It was time for me to heal my lingering self-doubts.

In short, my Montessori peers verbally attacked my abilities in the first couple months. This gave me the opportunity to seek out the truth. I pondered whether I was skilled enough for this endeavor, or were others' negative opinions about me accurate?

After a painful self-observation process, I concluded that these opinions about me were inaccurate. I was very skilled in the unique way of being from which I chose to come. I was sent to this new land not to be a clone of its inhabitants, but to forge new ground through a new approach. I did not come to merely teach facts, but to help guide the souls of children.

After I became confident in myself, others' doubts no longer impacted me as much. Your thoughts about yourself must always be the highest ones you hold. If you have any self-doubt, others will sense it; some may choose to attack you because of it. Do not see this as a negative thing, but as spirit's way of nudging you to heal any adverse opinions about yourself.

First impressions are hard to change, no matter how inaccurate. But during my first year of teaching, a child in my class nominated me anonymously for the Disney Teacher-of-the-Year award. In my Principal's end-of-the-year evaluation, I received the ranking of "exceeds standards"—the highest possible ranking. So you see, the truth is inside of you; it cannot be found in the opinions of others. All that matters are the opinions you hold about yourself.

When you enter into Canaan, you must rid yourself of the Canaanites, those lower-level thoughts lingering in your consciousness. You must develop a higher level of thoughts, particularly about yourself. When you can do this, you have defeated the inhabitants of Jericho—those thoughts that limited you. Jericho is the land where you rid yourself of the adverse notion that human intellect reigns supreme over spirit.[2] This adverse thought system is resistant to a change in leadership. When you defeat it in consciousness, you are ready to journey further in this new land. It takes about seven years before you arrive at a new sublevel of spiritual development, in the Promised Land.

In the Promised Land "...we have thirty-one kings (usurping thought forces) to conquer before we can peaceably settle down in our inheritance."[3] Think of these 31 kings as sub-stages in the Promised Land of spiritual development that your Joshua consciousness must overthrow to reach the Christ Consciousness stage of spiritual development.

These challenges will keep you actively working in the Promised Land, in whatever life area you are in, for the rest of your life. After you have conquered a new territory or sub-stage you will begin the journey of the soul again, originating in Egypt and concluding with your re-entrance back into the Promised Land at a higher sub-level of spiritual development.

Is it necessary to revisit the process again from the beginning? Yes, because the process through which consciousness evolves only occurs by journeying through all of the subsequent stages of spiritual development. Each time you take the journey of the soul, you acquire greater proficiency and mastery over the lessons taught in every stage of development. In this way you weed out any doubts and fears that linger in your subconscious mind, limiting your spiritual growth.

Before you are given more territory in the Promised Land, you must show you have evolved in consciousness. You will find revisiting the lands in your consciousness to be challenging still. However, it will not be quite as difficult as the first time you undertook the journey of the soul, because you will know what to expect.

You are usually in different stages of consciousness in different areas of your life. For example, you might be in the Wilderness stage in the life area of a personal relationship, while you are in the Promised Land stage regarding your career. At times you may work primarily on one area of your life; at others you may be assailed with work from all areas at once.

Why is it important to know where you are in consciousness in every area of your life? For me it made the journey easier. When I finally understood what was happening to me I became less scared, knowing it was of a spiritual nature.

I like to know what is needed to make spiritual progress as quickly as possible. Understanding the stages of development helps me know where I am at all times; it gives me an idea of how much further work is needed for advancement, in every area of my life. But the most important thing that knowing the stages of spiritual development gave me was a sense of comfort, peace, and confidence that a divine presence was in charge of my life. It was gratifying to know I was not just a random pawn, being moved around on a chessboard for the fun of it. Understanding the stages of spiritual development let me feel like a participant in the creation of my life.

Once again the spiritual stages of development are Egypt, Red Sea, Wilderness, Jordan River, Promised Land, and Christ Consciousness. The last two stages contain varying sub-stages. Where are you in the key areas of your life—your personal, professional, home life—and in the area of relationships, including one with yourself? Do you know? Do you care to find out? If not, why? Are you so satisfied with the conditions of your life that you choose to remain unconscious during its unfolding? Does finding out seem like too much work?

There is a tremendous amount of work involved. But it is the work that your soul came to Earth to do. Delaying the work by refusing to consciously engage in it will not make that work go away. The work of developing your soul will be waiting for you whenever you choose to start. Delaying will cost you valuable experiences, and keep you returning to the Earth plane more times than necessary. If you like the conditions of your life and you wish to return indefinitely to Earth re-creating the same thing, then do exactly what you are doing now: develop unconsciously. The day will come when you are no longer enjoying your life experiences here; then it will be time to evolve consciously. An unconscious life is a wasted life, devoid of valuable soul-altering opportunities for growth.

The journey of the soul is not a journey you have to take. In fact, very few people opt to do so, for a variety of reasons. If you can resist the call urging you to start the journey, then I suggest that you do so. This just means you are not ready to undertake the journey yet.

The journey is for people who have no other alternative but to heed their spirit's call, summoning them to take the journey. These people have been suitably awoken spiritually, and they cannot go back to sleep. If you are asleep, remain so—to awake is a dangerous thing for your ego, for you will be called to give up identification with it. This is not easy to do. Those who undertake the voyage from Egypt to the Promised Land are brave souls who are ready to pass into the next phase of spiritual evolution.

Are you ready? If not, this is a good place to put this book down and resume reading when you are ready. The challenge of conscious spiritual evolution is not for everybody; it is for people who are willing to do the necessary work.

For those who are willing: let us continue.

COMPASS

Why are you still playing at being small?

9

You Too Are God

I AM THAT I AM is the name God gave when asked his identity. This name acknowledged his existence, with no further explanation provided. We too exist: as an individualized aspect of God, yet one with the Creator at the same time. We are created in the image and likeness of God. All life is creative; thus, the purpose of our lives is to create using the divine gifts given to us by God. It is our responsibility to claim our inheritance as co-creators with God. We do this by arriving at the realization that we are part of the I Am, individual yet part of the divine whole. At the very center of our being is where this awareness lies. We connect with our I Am consciousness through a myriad of experiences while on Earth.

By not using your creative abilities, or by creating from the ego, you are cheating yourself of a life full of divine potential. It is not important *what* you create; what is important is that you *do* create. In order to create, you must first transcend the self-limiting thoughts you hold. You must come to the place where you can say, "I Am," with no more explanation needed. The thoughts that limit us are fears about our identity, worth, knowledge, ability, and so forth. We have addressed some of these concerns; now it is time to expand on others.

The biggest detriment to humankind is that we do not know our value. We value ourselves so little that we doubt our ability to create anything of real worth. In our false pursuit of humility, we learn to devalue ourselves. It is not necessary to downplay or deny your spiritual gifts; such denial honors neither you nor your gifts.

The true definition of humility is quiet appreciation and gratitude for our gifts. Humility is something easily felt when we understand the source of our divine gifts: God. They come from the source of all creation—why deny them? Could the problem be that we do not know where our gifts come from? Thus we are frightened, believing that we are the direct source of our gifts. If we believe we are our own source, then our feelings of unintelligence, helplessness, and fear are justified.

Quiet your fears! You are not the direct source of anything; the I Am that I Am is the direct source of all. There is no need to fear and quake with feelings of unworthiness. You are the vessel through which the I Am expresses. You are an individualized expression of God; deny this and you deny the truth about who you really are. What purpose does it serve to tremble like frightened children who do not know their spiritual identity? You are God's offspring. This makes you part of God, and God in your own right. What will you do with this information? Will you continue to deny your worth and value? How can you?—it was given to you by the I Am.

God seeks those willing to take a journey with the purpose of remembering who they really are. At times we learn who we really are by acting from states of being which do not reflect our true state of being: as spirit, that is. After doing this long enough, we eventually tire of this exercise in futility. Then we are ready to consciously experience who we really are through our actions, which are now aligned with our spiritual purpose. Now you and God can begin your work on Earth together.

The word "work" scares many people because it implies labor, difficulty, challenges, and so forth. But that is not the meaning of work in this context. "Work" now becomes that which you desire to do as a true expression of who you are. You no longer desire to work merely to create a living. Work now becomes a creative outpouring of your divine gifts, with the purpose of lifting your conscious experience of self to higher states of awareness. So work stops being what you *must do*, and instead becomes what you *desire to do* as a creative expression of yourself as God. Does that not sound better?

Another thing that frightens you is the thought that you too are God. In fact, this frightens you the most: you do not wish to accept your divinity. It is much easier to deny this truth, seeing yourself instead as a human being with limited or no power. Thinking of yourself as God frightens you to pieces. The word "God" has many connotations for you, many of them not pleasant: the parent in the sky, the overseer, the one who denies your dreams, and the one who allowed your loved ones to die. To many, God is the one who is indifferent to their suffering. All of these labels you have placed on God, yet God is none of these things. God, simply stated, is the source of all love. Love is the only true creative energy that exists in the Universe.

To identify with yourself as God is to know you are made up of only love, and to know that every other state is an illusion. Christ said that, of all of the gifts of spirit, the greatest of all is love. Love is who you are: it is your very nature. Love is something that can be felt and experienced.

You Too Are God

Envision your cells as organisms made up of little balls of light, vibrating at a speed so high that you literally cannot see them, but you can feel their energy. Love cannot be seen either, but its energy can be felt.

God is a God of love, and he uses that love to create. By this very definition, can you not see yourself as God? Are you any more comfortable with your Godhood now? It may take longer for some of you to accept this idea; that is okay. It does not matter if you are not ready to accept your true identity at this stage of your spiritual development. What *is* important is that you are acting out of—and using—the love you are made of to create whatever you desire to experience on Earth.

The act of creation probably never seemed relevant to you before now. What does it really mean to create? It means that you take seemingly nothing—neutral energy—and mold it into something substantive, giving it a concrete form. You can create whatever you choose, but it is imperative that you use your creative power. Create on a daily basis. Creation stimulates your higher self into action; the more you create, the more you are in touch with your spirit, and with the source of all creation. Creation is very important to God. He created you, and in doing so gave himself the ultimate creative experience. Give yourself the same gift. When your creation is before you, you too will understand what it is to be God.

Does it matter that the true source of your creative ability is God? It should, because if you are not the original source of creativity, you no longer have to fear losing your ability to create. You also do not have to be concerned about how good what you create is, in Earthly terms. How can you judge your creation when it is a reflection of the source? Who else can judge it? Others can choose to appreciate it or not—that is their right. But by what authority can they judge your creation?

Knowing that you are not the source of your creative talents should bring about profound relief, although it is important to understand that you too are part of the source. So, in essence, your creations have come from you as well. In the creation process, you will experience yourself as both creator and creative vessel at the same time. Creating allows God's spirit to flow through the empty space in your mind resulting from a lack of focused thoughts. The empty pathway in your mind establishes a connection between your spirit and God's. Out of this union comes inspiration, funneled through a unique vessel: you. The end result is your creation.

You can access your creativity from a place inside yourself at any time. You must invite creativity in. This is done by emptying yourself of thoughts and asking to be filled with the Holy Spirit, the usher of creativity. Do not do mental battle with the divine inspirations sent your way; accept them without judgment, and allow them to come through you. Only you can create in the unique way that spirit chooses to come through you. No two creative vessels can ever be exactly alike.

Let us talk a bit about the spirit. Identifying with the spirit as your true self takes a lot of work; it can be a painful process to let go of the ego. When you identify with yourself as spirit, your actions now come from a higher place. You are no longer programmed to automatically respond in ways conducive to your ego's needs and desires. At first, coming from a new place in being will seem disorienting. You will be mystified by the new ways you find yourself acting, and by the changes that these new actions bring about in your life. Nevertheless, you will hold true to the course of spirit. Why? Because you are now spirit more than anything else.

The realization of yourself as a spiritual being emerges at the end of the Jordan River stage, and continues in the Promised Land. Transitioning into spirit, I will repeat, is not an easy thing. Your new persona will seem startling. The best way to deal with your apprehension is to tell yourself the honest and bottom-line truth about what is happening. If you consciously challenge what you fear, you can transcend these feelings. The time will come when you must regularly act from the highest state of being, and stop choosing to act from lower states because it is easier or feels familiar. Two contradictory states cannot exist in the moment when it is time to act; you must choose one. Every time you choose spirit, you evolve. Remember: this is the work you have come to Earth to do.

Coming from the highest state of being possible while associating with others is even harder to do, particularly in the area of personal relationships. For most women, placing themselves first and acting from a place of self-love is quite challenging. Women do not like to hurt those they love; instead, they choose hurt for themselves, or allow themselves to constantly be hurt by another. This is not coming from a place of spirit. When you come from a place of spirit, you will put your self first; all others will become secondary figures in your life. It is not that you will now be hurting others; rather, you will be coming from a state of self-love first. Remember the commandment to "Love your neighbor as yourself." You cannot love another if you do not first love yourself.

This is what it means to be authentically self-loving: when those coming from a place of spirit love themselves first. If you are not used to practicing self-love, you might feel apprehensive at first because of all the momentous changes it will bring about in your life. You have to be honest with yourself: ask yourself what is really holding you back from acting from a place of self-love. Then you must determine if the changes you are making in your life come from a place of self-love and healing, or from someplace else.

After you ascertain the truth, you will understand what you must give up in consciousness in order to continue evolving. By naming your bottom-line fear you can exorcise it; consequently your outer circumstances will change as well. Sometimes the outer conditions in our lives might not change, but our way of dealing with them will. This is the only real change that can take place: the change in your behavior when you challenge and let go of an illusion held by your ego. You must be ready to accept the outer consequences of changing your behavior and acting in loving ways.

All actions have consequences—even the loving ones. When you act from a place of self-love, your action may cause the people, circumstances, or conditions in your life to change. This is the cause of your fear: although these people, circumstances, and conditions may not be the most loving things for you, you do not want them to go away. You are more comfortable with—more used to—pain and unloving conditions than with watching things and people move out of your life. You fear the unknown. You have to be willing to accept the outcome when unloving energy within you is surrendered for a higher vibration of love.

You are so content with what you settled for that you are not willing to let in anything higher—especially if it means facing an unknown future. What if that future is worse than what you have right now? The spirit does not operate from a place of fear; it operates out of love. So if you are feeling a lot of pain, know that it is not the real you experiencing that pain. The truth is, if you have the courage now to act from a place of spirit, you will give up illusions. It also means you are ready to accept the consequences of your spiritual actions—even if your ego is not.

It takes a long time before you are ready to take spiritual action. You must cross over in consciousness what seem to be millions of fearful thoughts before you are ready. Do not despair: your attempts are not in vain. It is more important to act authentically from your current level of consciousness than it is to change any outer condition or relationship. Most of us place a ridiculous amount of pressure on ourselves to be ready before we really are; this is self-defeating behavior. The quickest way to get ready to take some outer action is to accept wherever you are in consciousness, contentedly. When you can do better, you will. You must strive to create a worthwhile life for yourself: an authentic spiritual life. In order to do this, you must challenge and give up the illusions that have held your consciousness in captivity. These illusions have held you in bondage for far too long; your Moses consciousness is demanding that you let his people go.

Your life, up until this point, was created by and based on old beliefs you held about yourself; these beliefs do not serve you anymore. Accept the truth about your spiritual identity and create a new life from this truth. You are a child of God, worthy and deserving of the highest good. Accept this! Anything or anyone in your life that does not reinforce this truth must be released. In their place, you will be sent people and conditions that reflect the truth about who you authentically are: "a spiritual being having a human experience."

COMPASS

74

How does it serve your spirit to deny the authentic power you can access through it?

10

The Land Called Egypt

IN ORDER TO BECOME THE Christ you must first overthrow the interlopers in your consciousness. The Promised Land has 31 basic sublevels of development (kings), which you must overcome. When you have defeated all of them in consciousness in every life area, and have claimed all liberated territory for spirit, you will have reached the Christ Consciousness stage of development. In the Christ Consciousness stage you become the fully evolved Christ; the Earth platform is no longer necessary.

How long it takes to reach this point of spiritual development depends totally on you. Each choice you make—or do not make—creates a series of actions or events that form the basis of the work you will do on Earth. Making higher choices will ensure spiritual growth, and lower choices will keep you where you are in consciousness. The nature of your soul curriculum and how well you do depends on you. Not choosing to do any work to develop your soul is a choice as well, but this is only an option for a limited time: eventually there will be no other choice. The only alternative left will be the choice for the soul—everything else will have proven futile.

Let us revisit in more detail each stage of spiritual development you must master in order to reach Christ Consciousness. You had a lifetime to formulate your perceptions; changing them will not be easy. All that is asked is a willingness to see in a different way.

The first stage of development is Egypt. The main characteristic in Egypt is the pursuit of Earthly success. It does not matter the manner in which you go about this, or whether the achievement is of a personal, professional, educational, or physical nature. You are in Egypt at the stage of life when you are pursuing endeavors at the level of the material. In Egypt, the ego (your Pharaoh consciousness) reigns supreme. God has no judgment about you being in Egypt. He merely observes that some stages serve your spiritual growth better.

Do not despair about where you are in the moment in consciousness. Doing so is judging your consciousness as bad or insufficient in some way. Your consciousness creates your outer circumstances—you are where you need to be at each moment. This is a good thing, and it is the truth. The desire to seek higher forms of being, and higher states of consciousness, is inherent in your spiritual makeup. Disliking where you are in consciousness is counterproductive and will stifle any positive spiritual growth. In fact, the more you accept where you are now in consciousness, and make peace with it, the more readily you will evolve.

Egypt is the first stage of spiritual development, and it is a very important stage. The struggle for survival is important, albeit unnecessary. God promises you the survival basics. It seems ridiculous to most people to pursue the higher if you have no food to eat or place to live. This is understandable, so dealing with your basic survival needs in Egypt is necessary before moving on to higher pursuits. All that is required is that in the pursuit of these things, you are aware that God is the source of all.

Being in Egypt becomes a handicap when, instead of providing a good and basic level of material comfort, your mind becomes preoccupied with how to obtain increasingly high levels of material comfort. At what stage does your present material level become enough? You go from your parents' home to an apartment, to a townhouse, to a single-family starter house, to the house of your dreams, to an additional summer or weekend place. Then you dream about owning an estate. When is it enough?

The thought process in Egypt is one of more, more, and more. God holds no judgment on this: it is merely an observation. After your basic adult education has been acquired, you pursue degrees higher than the Bachelor's. Advanced degrees may be necessary for the type of work you do: you may need a higher-level degree to get a promotion and increased pay. You change jobs if you feel yours is not going anywhere, and you make this decision based solely on the financial rewards. You play the lottery.

The same mindset occurs in your personal life when you are in Egypt. You pursue relationships to find someone you think is the special, right person for you. When you find that someone, you strike up a conversation. This leads to friendship, dating, possibly living together, and ultimately marriage. At least half of these marriages will end in divorce. After a divorce or breakup, you start the cycle of searching all over again so you can begin with someone new.

I am not saying there is anything wrong with these material pursuits: that is what you are supposed to do in Egypt. These pursuits are merely time consuming. Your time and energies are focused on acquiring material things, which does not leave much room for any other pursuits, particularly spiritual ones. Seeking the material can keep you occupied for decades—even a lifetime.

People whose consciousness is in Egypt are preoccupied with the wellbeing of the Earthly body. Those in this stage of development spend a lot of time worrying about their physical appearance. People in Egypt appear to be outwardly successful. But if you look closely, past their illusory shell, these same people are usually spiritually empty, devoid of any real connection to their spirit. When looking directly in the eyes of a person in this stage of development, you cannot seem to connect to anything higher than what they project outwardly to the world.

Another characteristic of people in Egypt is that they find it hard to stay still for a long period of time. They must be in constant motion, and they have to go somewhere all of the time. Their mantra is, "I must do, do, and do some more." To those in Egypt, happiness is defined by activity, status, and material comforts.

If you talk to a person in the Egypt phase of spiritual development, they can list their many Earthly successes. If you ask them who they are, they usually respond by saying that they are a lawyer, businessperson, doctor, or whatever—you fill in the blank. They believe that what they *do* is indeed who they *are*. When a person offers their job title when asked who they are, their consciousness is still in Egypt.

Identifying yourself by what you do, instead of by your spiritual identity (as a child of God, for instance) is a good indicator of your stage of development. People in Egypt are passionate about many things, except for their spiritual development—they seem to have little interest in this area. Spirituality is an unknown entity to them.

The world is mostly filled with those in the Egypt stage of development. Again, this is neither a good thing nor a bad thing—simply an observation. People in the Egypt phase occupy industries and businesses worldwide. Their commitment to the pursuit of the material is what allows the world to operate, and to exist on the industrious level that it does. If we did not have people in this stage of development, we would not have many of the comforts that we take for granted.

People in Egypt provide services the world needs. But after our basic needs have been provided for, there is a higher way of being that needs to be sought out. Most people can stay happily in Egypt for the rest of their lives. However, an increasing amount of people are leaving Egypt. They left either voluntarily or are being forced out of Egypt by changing life circumstances.

In ancient Egypt, people were held in slavery for a time; their main job was to serve the ruling class or pharaoh of the time. Metaphysically, we understand this to be the time in our lives when we are enslaved to our own pharaoh or ruler—our ego. We work tirelessly to satisfy the dictates of our ego. In ancient Egypt, structures of worship were often built in the likeness of members of the Egyptian ruling class. Thus, their image or ego became the false idol that they began to worship. Held in the collective consciousness of the human species is the archetype of servitude to the ego, and worship of its false ideals.

It is interesting that many of the structures built in ancient Egypt still exist today. They are rooted firmly on the foundations they occupy. Are not our mental structures that we built to worship the ego still standing as well? There is much we can learn from ancient times that is quite useful in our own spiritual journey, if understood from a spiritual or metaphorical viewpoint. See yourself in the characters and situations of old, as recounted in the Bible and other holy books. By making a connection in your own life to the stories and lessons taught, you view them metaphorically. When you make a connection to lessons and stories of a spiritual nature and understand that they offer a higher meaning in consciousness than just a literal one, you are viewing them metaphysically.

The truth is, most of the slaves in Egypt did not truly want to be liberated. Oh, they whined and complained like most of us do when we are under the whip of labor. But they simply wanted to be delivered from having to serve the material needs of the ruling class. They sought to exchange their old bonds for new ones—this time willingly engaging in servitude to satisfy their own material desires. This is not true liberation, because materiality is still the God being served. The captors had merely changed. When we exchange thoughts of materiality that limit us in consciousness merely for more of the same, we are still not free.

The Hebrew slaves prayed to God to set them free, but it took many hundreds of years for their prayers to be answered. The delay was partly due to insincerity. We idly complain about our work and other conditions we would like to change. But it takes a long time before we are truly ready to invoke change in our lives. God knows this and waits until we are sick and tired of being sick and tired. Then he sends a deliverer to his people to guide their way out of Egypt. He sends forth our Moses consciousness.

Moses, after awakening in our consciousness, can deliver us out of Egypt. Many people erroneously assume that only one race of people has been chosen to enter into the Promised Land. This race of people should be commended for being one of the first to heed God's call and undertake the journey of the soul. We owe them our gratitude. They showed us the way to the Promised Land, and they should be highly praised for doing so.

You will find in every religion that a similar journey has been undertaken by the central figures in each doctrine. Anyone can be chosen. Those who come to God in earnest and who work diligently to develop their spiritual faculties should consider themselves chosen. The land that they will reach in consciousness as a result of their spiritual labors will become their own Promised Land. Feelings of resentment when you believe that others are chosen instead of you stem from burying your own call to journey deep within you. God invites all of us to undertake the journey of the soul; those of us who accept his invitation are the chosen ones.

There is no other deliverer coming to save us—we must save ourselves. In ancient Egypt, Moses showed us how. We are held in captivity by our slave mentality, which is primarily focused on the material. We decide how long we will remain captive to this mentality. We complain and beseech God to deliver us from captivity. But as he did with the slaves in ancient Egypt, God will not answer our cries until he knows that we are ready to move. To be moved in consciousness, that is.

Moses, the deliverer, is a liberated thought that has broken free from the lower-level thoughts that plague our minds when we are in Egypt. Our lower thoughts hold us in captivity, making slaves out of us. They hold us in bondage, forcing us to serve their agenda. But we do so voluntarily. We can choose to withdraw our servitude to them at any time.

A Moses thought could be a desire or dream we cherish. For example, when we are having a bad day, when we are feeling down, our Moses thought could be a daydream about quitting our job and doing the kind of work that we truly desire. This thought might cheer us up for a while. But when we are feeling better, we typically return it to the back recesses of our mind. We then resume our routine and old way of thinking.

These daydreams come from Moses, our liberator, who is held in the back of our consciousness until we call him forth. The vast numbers of thoughts occupying our conditioned minds are about why we cannot quit our job. We think about our dependency on a paycheck, and how we are going to pay our bills. These fearful, worrisome, and doubting thoughts are the ones that enslave us. Are we waiting to be set free by a deliverer other than ourselves?

When your deliverer, Moses, can no longer be held comfortably in the back of your consciousness, and its thought system is propelled to the forefront, you are ready to be delivered out of Egypt. At this time your Moses consciousness, a new emerging spiritual thought system, will instantly be confronted by feelings of unworthiness. Pharaoh, the present ruler of your consciousness, will resist any attempt to usurp him. Another name for pharaoh—other than ego—is fear.

Who will win the battle in your consciousness between Moses (your deliverer) and Pharaoh (the ruler of your mind)? It remains to be seen. Moses seeks to free you from lower thoughts of fear that hold you in bondage to the material. You will be sent many miracles, which will help to loosen the stronghold of your Pharaoh consciousness. Pharaoh will deny the miraculous nature of them and call them coincidences. He will conjure up his own versions of God's miracles. The difference is that the miracle that God is giving to you comes from an authentic place of power; whereas the ego attempts to conjure up a miracle based on false power.

What holds people in bondage the most, and limits their ability to take any action, is dependency on a paycheck. People worship their paycheck, crediting it as the source of their prosperity. God is the true source of our prosperity—a paycheck is merely a channel through which we receive it. Aside from work, you can be enslaved by the worship of the "Mrs." that may come before your last name. There is also the false idol we have created in the form of home mortgages—and let us not forget the idol of luxury cars. My personal favorites are the idols called comfort and routine.

This is what worshipping false idols means; will you allow your servitude to the material to hold you in captivity forever? Whatever the name of the false god you serve, you continue to do so because you refuse to stop acting like little children fascinated with toys. Are you ready to allow your Moses consciousness to free you from the bonds of slavery that hold you captive in Egypt?

The answer solely depends on where you are in consciousness. Are you tired of Egypt? Did it turn out to be what you hoped for and expected? Did it fill the empty spaces inside of you, or do you still feel empty? Is your soul rising up against being held in slavery for so long? Is there a stirring, a longing for something more, that you are finding harder and harder to ignore? Is Moses demanding that you let his people go? Has it become less painful for you to take action than to do nothing? If the answers to all of these questions are yes, you are ready to be delivered out of Egypt.

If none of these conditions apply to you, then you are where you need to be in consciousness. I am talking to those to whom these conditions apply, and who are ready to be moved in consciousness. Your internal guide, Moses, will help free you from bondage; he will help you enter your own Promised Land, the land of your dreams. But Moses can only work through you. It takes courage, faith, and a sense of adventure to leave Egypt. If you are still largely conflicted about whether or not to act, you must make up your mind. Who is to be the ruler in your consciousness: Pharaoh or Moses?

Who will win the battle in your consciousness between Moses (your deliverer) and Pharaoh (the ruler of your mind)? Why do you think so?

11

The Voyage Over the Sea

WHEN YOU GO AGAINST THE standard norms of the world, you will be *crucified* for it. Any aberration in the flock holds the potential for dissent in the rank of thoughts that hold us captive. When somebody deviates from the agreed-upon norms in society, they are attacked by others. Those who attack do so in order to assuage feelings of regret, fear, and guilt over having ignored their own Moses consciousness when it repeatedly called for them to depart Egypt. They think, "who are you, to do what we were afraid to do?" When you remain within the limits of societal conditioning, others feel better about themselves and their lower-level choices. This explains the viciousness of the attacks against you when you decide to follow Moses out of Egypt.

The attacks will come from those closest to you: your spouse, family, friends, children, and co-workers. The thoughts of those closest to you cannot liberate you—you can only liberate yourself by following your own indwelling guide. You may lose the support and respect of some of the people in your life. You may have to end your association with those who are not willing to grant you the freedom to evolve in consciousness. Surprisingly, you may discover those who you thought would be your biggest critics turn out to be your greatest allies.

There is no reason to end all relationships with people who do not support you, or who criticize your decision to take a journey of the soul. You are only affected by their attacks because of the fear that besieges you when you decide to initiate the journey. You fear that others might be right. You should play it safe, or be what holds you in bondage the most: practical. What actually is practicality? It is a word invented by those who choose the ego's reasoning over the spirit's urging.

You cannot be waylaid by those who attack you at this time in your life. You must offer them a silent blessing, and recognize that their mentality is still held captive in Egypt. You must focus on liberating yourself from anything within that still can be affected by others' negative opinions: then you will truly be free.

Freedom is an inner state we reach. Being externally free from problems, people, and circumstances is not true freedom. These things cannot always be controlled by you. True freedom comes from liberating your consciousness, which in fact is what is keeping you enslaved. Others' opinions about your choices will diminish after you accept and make internal peace with your decisions.

When you have been freed from captivity from your Pharaoh consciousness that held you in bondage in Egypt, you will then have to cross over the Red Sea. At the very time that you decide to act or move forward in consciousness, you will be overcome and beset by fear—mostly fear of the unknown. If you cave in now, your journey will end

The Voyage Over the Sea

here. Know that if you decide to persevere, Moses will deliver you safely across the Red Sea of terror that still lies within your consciousness.

Crossing over the Red Sea may look different in each of our lives. The journey is essentially about evolving into a new, unknown way of being. Eradicating all of your fearful thoughts could take a lifetime—or many lifetimes. God uses your Moses consciousness to clear a path through the center of your fearful thoughts. It is cleared long enough for you to be temporarily liberated from your fears, and for you to arrive at a place of higher awareness. Your old and fearful thoughts cannot go with you into this new land; they must remain behind in Egypt.

You may choose initially to remain attached to some old aspects of your life that you are not yet ready to fully release. What does this look like? One might choose to stay connected, for a time, with people or conditions that still remain in Egypt. This happens because the old still feels familiar, and because you have not yet fully developed into a higher state of consciousness.

Not everyone is discontented with their jobs, lives, relationships, marriages, bodies, economic conditions, and so forth. In fact, some of us are quite content with these things. For those who are not, these words are for you: Will you not allow them to stir within you the awakened truth? You must take action! To know the truth and not to live it is a sin. The metaphysical definition of sin is "missing the mark." You miss the mark when you do not act on your truth.

You ponder whether or not your truth is correct. Your truth is true for you, and does not have to meet anyone else's standard of correctness. In fact, be prepared: more likely than not, your truth will not be believed by anybody else but you. If you depend on validating your beliefs through others' acceptance of them, you will be disappointed. Creation is not dependent on others holding the same beliefs as you. Creation emerges out of what *you* believe. What you believe, you then create.

After you have crossed over the Red Sea into the Wilderness, your consciousness can never again return fully to the place from which it evolved. Although you were excited about commencing your journey, this excitement will only sustain you for a short while. As soon as you enter the Wilderness stage of development, your excitement will change into doubt and confusion. You bring baggage from Egypt in your consciousness with you when you enter the Wilderness, and you must learn to set it aside.

COMPASS

How do people in Egypt seek to keep you there in bondage?

12

Becoming One with Silence

WHO ARE YOU IN RELATION to the nonmaterial? You will find out in the Wilderness. When you leave Egypt and cross through the Red Sea, you enter into the next stage of your journey. The Wilderness stage of consciousness has been given many names by many different people. Some refer to parts of it as the "Dark Night of the Soul," a term made famous by St. John of the Cross. To learn more about this phenomenon, read *Putting on the Mind of Christ* by Jim Marion.[1] Some people may believe that you are clinically depressed in this stage of development.

These descriptions might frighten you, but the Wilderness level of development is a very challenging one. At this stage in consciousness you have to shed—or rid yourself of—identification with the ego as your true self. This is a painful process for most to endure. The identity you erroneously believe to be you, must be given up at this time.

Most people are attached to material possessions. To be asked to give up material things theoretically, in consciousness, is one thing. Being asked to give up material things in our physical reality is quite another. If you knew that you might lose your home, car, and material possessions in the Wilderness stage, would you still proceed? It bears repeating that there is nothing wrong with materiality: God does not judge how much or little people desire materiality in their lives. The purpose of the Wilderness is not to lose your material possessions—the purpose is to seek a higher state of being.

When your attention is no longer focused on something, it falls by the wayside. The same thing happens to your material possessions when you begin to focus on spirit for the first time, and to see yourself as something other than a human personality. The loss of possessions is not a punishment, but a byproduct of a lack of attention on the material.

Now, I realize that many of us did not consciously make this decision to depart with the material. It was forced upon you, or so you would argue. I ask you: was it really forced? Did any part of you hate your life circumstances (over a long period of time), and pray to be delivered from them? Yet, when you were liberated from them, it seemed like punishment instead. The story has not been written yet—in fact, it is now only beginning. How you choose to perceive what has happened to you will make all the difference in how things will go.

As the material fades away, you learn that the most important question in your life becomes who you are in relation to the nonmaterial. Will you still feel like you when you are no longer working, no longer in a relationship, or no longer living a certain lifestyle? The answer is yes. You will feel like you, but like a new and improved you. You will feel more alive, more energized, and more at peace than ever before. How can this be, you will wonder, when you are not out in the world, doing? It is simple: when you remove the outer distractions in your life, you will have room for yourself. Your true self, that is.

The Wilderness stage of development is not about loss—it is about liberation. You are liberated from the bondage of attachment to outer things. After attachment has been removed, you are truly free to enjoy the material in a detached way. You will no longer see possessions as reflections of yourself. They will simply be possessions. The purpose of the Wilderness is to know yourself as you are, not as you imagine yourself to be. You begin the search for your true identity.

But whom can you trust to show you who you really are? Can you trust the same you that decided you were a human personality and lived life accordingly? No, you cannot. All visions of you other than God's have been tainted by the ego, and as a result cannot be trusted. Ask God to share his vision of you, and accept it when he gives it. In this way you can get a true picture of who you really are.

The search for your true identity leads to God. God is found in the silence that you tune into inside of yourself. For in silence, God can be heard clearly. God still can be heard despite the mental chatter which sounds like static in your mind, but it is difficult. Silence is required to obtain the frequency necessary to reach God. The Wilderness stage of development allows you to know your Creator for the first time in a tangible way. God is in you, a silent presence in the background, watching and waiting until you acknowledge his or her presence.

The Wilderness stage of development is a metamorphic stage. You are shedding your old skin and becoming something new that you do not yet understand. As women know, birth can be quite a painful experience, yet at the same time it can be beautiful. That is how you will find your experience in the Wilderness: agonizing and yet beautiful. The agony comes from fearful thoughts about your physical survival, thoughts that plague you on a daily basis. The beauty comes from having freedom to do whatever you wish. You have the freedom to creatively fill each day in any way you choose.

In the Wilderness you will spend a lot of time being quiet and still. Hours will stretch before you like the sands in the desert, countless in number. At times, each minute will feel even longer than the previous one. The purpose of being still for such a long period of time, initially for up two and a half years, is to get you to the place where you begin to transcend the limits of time.

Time in the Wilderness becomes your first lesson on existing in the now. In the Wilderness, an experience of now is all you have. To learn more about the importance of living in the now, read *The Power of Now* by Eckhart Tolle.[2] Your preoccupation and obsession with tomorrow must be surrendered. You will not be ready to depart the Wilderness until you have transcended the notion of time being a hindrance. You are then ready to see time as a tool that serves you. When you see time as a tool you use to bring about healing in the Wilderness, you will understand why the stay here is lengthy.

How does the Wilderness serve as a healer? By the time you have entered the Wilderness stage, you will have sustained a plethora of emotional injuries and wounds. If visible, they would resemble the wounds left from gunshots, covering every inch of your body. The impact of each bullet (negative experience) left a gaping hole in your psyche, one that has never been fully healed. How long can you live drowning in the tides of your own pain? Will you never stop to repair the damage? Will you continue to deny its very existence?

This is what the Wilderness is for: to undergo intensive surgery on your emotional psyche. You will have an opportunity to feel fully all of the pain that has ever wounded you up until this point in your life. You will get in touch with the wounds within you that have never fully healed. You will feel this pain all at once. It will be an intense experience, and somewhat debilitating. This is the reason you will stay still and spend so much time in silence: you are healing. Contrary to popular opinion, in order to heal pain, you must allow yourself to feel it first. You cannot heal what you do not first allow yourself to feel. Allow yourself to feel the pain within you.

The pain will seem quite bottomless at times. But this is an illusion: there is an end to it. When exactly you reach it depends on how much pain needs to be healed within you, and on how long it takes you to heal. I myself had a good amount of pain to be healed, and I healed relatively slowly. The good news is that after the pain has healed, it is gone for good. You will never suffer from these wounds again. You may suffer from new wounds, but not from the old, healed ones.

People are terrified to feel their pain. They feel it will overwhelm them. It will for a while—but only for a while. If you do not feel your pain, and allow it to flow through you and empty out of you, it will poison you and you will not heal. It will poison you to the point where you will become physically ill. This is one consequence of not healing your emotional wounds at an early enough stage, before disease sets in.

If you do not make time to heal, healing will come to you on its own accord. But not before it first brings disease in its wake. Disease and illness come in order to draw attention to unhealed wounds within you. What if bullets, or a partial fragment of them, were allowed to stay in your body indefinitely? While this is a dramatic description, your emotional wounds deserve the same attention a gunshot wound would receive. Death in some form or another is imminent if immediate action is not taken. The death of the ability to come from a place of love within you is one consequence you might experience.

The Wilderness is a place where your spirit calls you to heal. Healing the wounds that are damaging you becomes the highest priority in your life—everything else must fall by the wayside. Not being consciously aware that you are wounded is no excuse. On some level you must be aware that you are in pain, and that this pain adversely affects the true expression of yourself as spirit on Earth. There is no higher work to be done than healing your own wounds. What good are you to another if you are as wounded as they? Some people's pain is buried so deeply that they deny its existence; they are not consciously aware of it. If they spent one week in silence, the amount of pain that would arise would be staggering.

How do you heal your wounds? The first step is to allow yourself to feel the pain associated with them. Pain will not kill you; avoidance of it might. Pain is not endless, but transitory: it changes from one state to another. Pain, when transformed, becomes a great healer. It is important for you to understand that *you* are not in pain—not the true you, your spirit. Your human personality is what is in pain, because of the countless emotional wounds it has sustained.

After healing, the place within you that used to be filled with pain is empty. You were filled with emotional poison that was creating blockage within you. As a result, there was no room within you to consciously come in contact with your spirit. The unoccupied space within that you have freed up creates a place for spirit to flow through you. The emptier you become after the removal of blocked energy within, the more quickly you will become filled with spirit. Some people choose to fill their healed spaces with new wounds and pain by refusing to learn lessons that their spirit is seeking to teach them. When old wounds have healed, you at least have the option of deciding how you want to fill the empty space within.

You come to the Earth with a limited amount of energy. If most of your energy is blocked as a result of unresolved issues and pain, you cannot use it. The energy within most people is in this condition. Can you not see why people are languishing, figuratively speaking? They lack energy—the energy of the spirit. Yes, energy is boundless, tireless, and infinite, but only if it is allowed to circulate freely, regenerating itself. Every time energy is holed up within you because of unresolved pain, you prevent that part of yourself from evolving into a higher state of consciousness.

Let me explain further. Picture a ball of light, around the size of a grape. The light begins circulating and moving at a certain speed all around you; suddenly it faces an obstacle it cannot move through, so it comes to the obstruction and abruptly stops. It cannot move any further—it just remains there. Then you see another ball of light and the same thing happens. Eventually most of the balls are stuck in midair, unable to move ahead or backwards.

This is the state you find yourself in when you refuse to heal your pain: a state of being stuck. You are holding back a sphere of light, or love that is seeking to heal you. Light and love must be allowed to flow unrestricted throughout your body. As it flows through you, all else flows out of you. The light is a healer: it comes to liberate you from the consequences of holding onto pain in any form.

Think of light as spheres of energy moving around you in a circular motion. A ball of light that is allowed to move around within you joins in likeness with other balls of lights inside you. When one ball of light joins another it grows in size, and the sphere of light becomes larger. What would happen if all the balls of light were allowed to move around you in that way, always moving and never stopping? I will tell you: you would cease to exist in physical form. You would transcend to a higher plane of consciousness. The individual spheres of light, after coalescing into one sphere of light, would accelerate your consciousness high enough for you to leave the physical dimension.

Why are we talking about spheres of light? A sphere is a circle, and a circle has neither beginning nor end. A sphere of light is circulatory in nature and encloses what it travels around. Light is energy. Energy is a physical manifestation of an idea produced from and out of love—you might say that energy is love in form. If a ball of energy, or love in form, is allowed to enclose or surround any wound or problem, it will heal it.

Light is a healing energy of love originating from the source of all love: God.

God sends you light to heal you. But God can only heal what you allow to be healed through you. Delay no more: allow the energy of healing within you. You must get yourself out of the way of your healing; rid yourself of fear of the healing process. The only way to combat this fear is to usher in self-love and self-compassion. As light surrounds your wounds, it will heal them using the energy of love, and the pain you feel will disintegrate. The vacuum, the pocket of empty space freed up from healed wounds, is now ready to be filled with the divine energy of love.

The work of healing pain will be done in the Wilderness phase of spiritual development. Being still, refraining from outer activities, will enable inner healing to occur. You are not being asked to meditate and remain silent all day long, but most of you will want to engage in some form of routine meditation during this period. The more you are in touch with the divine Creator within you, the more quickly you will heal.

Once again, feeling pain is the thing that most humans abhor the most. We overeat, take drugs, use sexual energy destructively, verbally attack others, and perpetuate violent acts, all in an effort to avoid feeling pain. This is because you think you *are* the pain that you are feeling.

Your pain and you are not one and the same. Pain exists separately from the real you. Pain is energy: it is energy gone horribly wrong. Pain stems from a negative reaction to something that occurs in your life. It is your emotional reaction to what occurs. You are also not your emotions, as literature such as Don Miguel Ruiz's book *The Mastery of Love*[3] has taught. Read it—it fully explains the phenomena of the pain body and the emotional body. What you will learn is that you have a choice about whether or not to allow yourself to identify with pain. Instead, you learn to build a case for love and its offshoots: peace and healing.

Can you connect to any part of you that feels as though it's dying? Who do you think is really dying, and why?

13

Different Aspects of Yourself

YOU ARE NOT YOUR PAIN, nor are you your emotions. The best time to be aware of this is when you are experiencing pain of an emotional nature. The real you—your spirit—does not exist on the same plane of existence as your emotions. If you are consciously aware of this when experiencing pain, you can become the observer or witness to the pain that an aspect of you is feeling. This separates you further from identifying with the pain as the totality of your experience. If you are an observer of your emotional reactions when experiencing pain, you will realize that two aspects of yourself exist at the same time, and that each has a different reaction to painful stimuli.

One aspect of yourself is observing another: the aspect that is in pain. The aspect doing the observing does so in a detached and unemotional way; it knows the pain that part of you is simultaneously feeling is not authentic. It is merely the ego's reaction to losing power because of the shattering of its closely held beliefs.

This aspect of yourself is the higher you. You must learn to identify and unite with this higher part of yourself during painful situations. Try and do so in the first three seconds of any emotional encounter that you deem painful. You are not being asked to become detached and unemotional when in pain, but to observe that a part of you already is detached, while at the same time another part of you believes itself to be in emotional pain.

Expressing emotions is normal and healthy. If you allow yourself to express emotions early when you have a painful experience, you will expedite the process of healing. To reiterate: when you experience a situation you find painful, there is a part of yourself that is detached, observing another aspect of yourself that is in pain. In essence, it seems that two of you exist: the observer and the reactor.

Why is this knowledge valuable or useful? It's because if two aspects of yourself exist, you now have a choice. You do not have much of an option when there is only one choice, but you have now been given two. You can also choose to oscillate back and forth between these two aspects, identifying with both simultaneously or in turn. You can also choose not to identify with either of these aspects.

You must now make a choice. Which aspect of yourself will you choose to identify with? It depends on how you see yourself in relation to pain: as its victim, its observer, or its creator. In essence, you are all three. You are the human personality experiencing the pain. You are the soul observing your experience, and you as spirit are the creator of your experience.

You create and draw to you what you most need to learn, as taught in *Conversations with God*. What you may not recognize is that in all of your experiences, you have the option to decide which aspect of yourself you

Different Aspects of Yourself

want to identify with. Going to the movies is an example of this, one that is used often in spiritual jargon. You are the observer of the movie that you are watching. You can also be a character in the movie, the one taking part in or experiencing the drama. You can also be the director, directing yourself in a movie that you will later watch—in this role you are the creator of the movie.

There is a fourth aspect of you as well. Who is the fourth you? It is the aspect of yourself that is neither the doer, the observer, nor the creator of your experiences. The fourth aspect of you is God.

God is the fourth aspect of your divine nature. To review: the first aspect is your human personality, or the one who experiences the events. The second aspect is your soul, or the one who observes your human personality. The third aspect is your spirit, or the creator of the events, circumstances, or people in your life. The final aspect, the fourth you, is God showing up as you. God shows up as you—or, in actuality, you show up as God. This happens after you join in union with the divinity that exists inside of you.

To merge into oneness with God is to surrender individual and isolated thoughts that you have kept separate from the I Am. When you no longer see yourself and God as separate entities, and you become one in conscious awareness, you have become one with God. When you reach this stage of consciousness, you will be in the fourth state of being: you will have the experience of knowing yourself as God.

This level of consciousness is rarely seen on the Earth plane. It is a state of being that is reached on a realm of existence higher than Earth. It will occur in a dimension that you return to after you shed your physical body. Whatever you choose to call that dimension is up to you. It is, however, a higher dimension than the one you exist in now. It holds increasing levels of awareness that lead to the ultimate experience of becoming fully aware of you as part of God.

To know yourself as a soul is the typical level of spiritual development you will obtain on Earth. Knowing yourself as a soul means that you experience yourself as both a human personality and a spirit. You identify with both forms of being, and oscillate between them. To know yourself as spirit is to only have one point of reference that you identify with. There no longer exists within you any other aspect, such as a human personality, that you identify with or come from. This is challenging to accomplish while still on Earth.

The Wilderness is the stage in consciousness where you first realize that another you exists. When you cease focusing on the needs of the human personality, you gradually stop identifying with it; this allows another you to emerge. In the Wilderness you will find your soul. Your soul is the part of you that becomes aware of your spirit. It is already aware of your human personality, but it awakens to a new part of itself in the Wilderness. The soul becomes aware of a part of itself that simply *is*. It exists simply in a state of being and pure awareness. This pure awareness can be accessed through meditation, or when the mind is awake and free of thoughts.

This quiet awareness starts to emerge in the Wilderness. After an initial stage of resistance, this awareness becomes your preferred state of being—so much so that in the Wilderness stage you do not want to do too many activities or go out too often. You want to spend your time being quietly aware. When you first come into conscious contact with your soul, you are so filled with the awakened you that nothing else matters to you but remaining in this energy. After first contact with this alien part of yourself, you delight in the experience—though at the same time, your soul identifies with the human part of you that worries about bills, money, and physical survival. In the Wilderness you constantly go back and forth between the two aspects of yourself, until you start to identify with one more than the other.

Different Aspects of Yourself

In the Wilderness you are taught dependency on God. You can no longer depend on yourself to provide for your physical needs; you have voluntarily chosen to give up focus on those needs for a while, in order to remain still. Here you start to know God as the source of all. This is very difficult to do, because you are so used to depending on yourself for everything. How lonely it must have been for you, believing that only you could provide for and take care of yourself! Did you not know that there is a power far greater than any we can access by ourselves—one that is willing to take care of us? If we allow it to, in co-creation with us, it will do so.

In biblical times, when the Hebrew people were freed from slavery in Egypt and entered the Wilderness, God provided sustenance for them. He sent manna, which fell from the sky for them to eat. But many people had trouble believing that their sustenance would come again on the next day. Because of their fears, they hoarded some of the bread received that day, to eat tomorrow. They quickly realized that when they tried to eat the hoarded manna the next day, it had decayed. Sustenance received one day will not sustain you for long on subsequent days.

This is very much like when you achieve a high level of spiritual awareness. In one day you acquire sustenance from prayer, meditation, or by doing spiritual activities. Then the next day you try to access your previous supply of sustenance, without first doing the work necessary to acquire it anew. You are trying to get daily bread from yesterday's harvest. If you choose not to do the daily spiritual work needed to join in union with spirit, you will go without the inner resources that spirit provides for you on that given day—and on every day that you do not reconnect anew with spirit.

Spirit must be accessed daily. This is the way manna or sustenance is given to you. God never stopped sending manna to those of us in the Wilderness—we stopped believing that we could receive it. We must obtain our supply of manna daily during the Wilderness stage of spiritual development.

You cannot maintain a storehouse of spiritual sustenance if you do not fill it daily by doing some form of spiritual activity. This storehouse is your consciousness filled with positive thoughts. In the Wilderness phase, you will develop the daily practice of filling your storehouse and calling forth enough sustenance to get you through that day. You will live one day at a time; you only receive from spirit what you need to get you through that day, with nothing left over for tomorrow. In this way your consciousness will be trained to go to the source of all on a daily basis. If we could remain filled with spirit, without having to first fill up with it daily, what would be the motivation to access spirit on a regular basis?

The Wilderness is a challenging stage of conscious development. How many of us depend on our paychecks or bank accounts as our sources of money? What do you do when your bank account says zero, and there is no longer any money coming in every two weeks? You have the opportunity to find out when you are in the Wilderness. I say "opportunity" because this series of experiences is not a punishment. It is an opportunity to develop a faith-filled consciousness, dependent on God for your good.

That is not to say that you should not work: in the Wilderness phase you are doing a different *kind* of work. You are working on your spiritual development, as opposed to being out in the world. After you leave the Wilderness you will resume working in the world in a new way, one more aligned with your spiritual nature.

The Wilderness is a place where you get the bugs out of your system, so to speak. The bugs are the thought patterns—for example, your fears—that limit you from developing your divine potential. You will have an opportunity to experience your fears so you can transcend them firsthand in the Wilderness. Any amount of fear that is eradicated in consciousness justifies the time you spend in the Wilderness.

In the Wilderness you are no longer very concerned about your physical appearance. You are typically sloppy to a high degree, your outer environment reflecting the disorder and chaos in your inner environment. You feel so out of control that it is no wonder your outer environment reflects this as well. You cannot find the strength or interest to clean, or to organize anything to any significant degree. You are often literally surrounded by piles of junk: clothes, books, papers, magazines, and so forth.

You feel ashamed of the condition of your outer environment, but you cannot yet find the energy to do anything about it. When you begin to heal internally, the obstructions that keep you stuck mentally and prevent you from taking outer action will be removed. After you create internal order in your mind and consciousness, external order will follow suit.

Maybe you can identify with someone going through this experience. The extent of outer chaos in their lives is directly proportional to the amount of pain they are presently experiencing. Do not judge them—you are not aware of what is going on with them internally. If you are affected by their external disorder, do as much as you possibly can to keep it from disturbing you. Contributing to the guilt felt by someone undergoing this experience will help neither the individual nor you. In fact, an additional element of embarrassment to deal with will delay their healing even further.

The outer condition of one's environment is often an indication of their inner environment. The outer disorder of material items is a reflection of inner turmoil. An environment that is sterile, cold, and empty in nature, or pretentious and filled with too many material items, can symbolize a person's inner consciousness as well.

When you are going through the Wilderness experience, it is far easier if you go through it alone, with just yourself as witness to your pain. However, this is often not the case; you might be living with people or are in relationships with others around you. Their judgments will burden you further, at the time when you least need it. You must be aware that you cannot see what they see from the outside; all you can identify with is the great internal pain you are feeling. Understanding on both sides is needed.

In the Wilderness you air all of your dirty laundry, so to speak. But you are airing it with the purpose of cleaning and healing it. You cannot do this effectively if you must take on the disapproval and expectations of others who cannot stand to witness the external evidence of your pain. Be of good courage and know that this stage will not last forever. Your wounds must be revealed before they can be healed.

The Wilderness stage comes to you at a time when you are ready to heal, unable to move any further in life until you do so. How long you stay in the Wilderness is entirely up to you. You must liberate yourself from identifying with the human personality and begin to know yourself as a spiritual being. If you delay doing what is necessary spiritually, either because you do not know what to do or because you are unwilling to do it, your stay in the Wilderness may be lengthy. Knowledge is crucial to liberation: understanding where you are, and what you need to do at every stage of your conscious evolution, will make the journey easier.

The Wilderness is a testing ground of sorts. It tests your ability to do the hard work of healing the emotional pains and wounds you have accumulated up until this point in your life. Remaining wounded prohibits you from moving forward in consciousness. You can continue to deny that what is occurring in your life at this point has anything to do with spirit, and thus circumvent the lessons that must be learned. But you will quickly learn the futility of your efforts, since you will be unable to manifest anything you desire or need. The power you once had in Egypt—to manifest successfully—is now gone. The ego is rendered powerless in the Wilderness.

Henceforth all external power comes from an internal source: God. You realize that real, lasting change cannot be made without co-partnering with God in creation. You stop seeing things from a perspective of "I," and instead start seeing from the perspective of we, meaning "God and I." In the Wilderness you will learn you can no longer do anything without the assistance of God. This is a great thing, in fact—it enables you to create from a place of true spiritual power.

What are your fears about permanently surrendering your will to God?

14

Filling the Empty Space

GOD HAS NO DESIRE TO control you, or the decisions you make, in any way. What would be the purpose of that, when the I Am has given you free will? God's desire is that you learn the most effective way to create a desirable life for yourself. If you are going about something in an ineffective way, is it not a loving act to point this out and show you a higher way of creating? The highest way to create is to allow the I Am to create through you and with you.

Before this can happen, healing must first take place within you. You need to heal the pain your human personality has undergone: pain that is adversely affecting you. When you experience pain, emotions become stymied and you are no longer able to come from a place of love inside you. Instead you feel unworthiness, fear, hurt, bitterness, resentment, shame, doubt, and self-hate. These are false states. Your spirit does not identify with these emotions—yet your soul experiences these false states on a regular basis.

When do you heal all of the wounds overflowing with poison that, if acknowledged, would rise up in you like a river whose dam had burst? The poison within you, if not healed, eventually transforms itself into a physical ailment of some kind. If you are spiritually aware, you will see the ensuing illness as a warning; you will take some sort of spiritual action to heal the emotional pain that is poisoning you.

Do you believe that emotional pain, if felt deeply enough, produces no significant consequences in its host? Is that rational? You are not your emotions—but your emotions are part of your experience, and the effect they can have on you is quite real. You have stored experiences you deem painful in your psyche, untreated for many years. Treating any wound is painful. But the Wilderness is a place where you must allow your emotional wounds to be healed.

Denying that you are in a state of unbearable pain will catch up with you in the long run. You will be the one who has to pay the costly penalty that continuous denial brings. The origin of any physical disease can be traced back to a breach in an individual's emotional body. Heal an emotional wound internally, at the level of emotions, and it will not manifest into an external physical disease.

Do all physical diseases result from untreated internal states of turmoil? What about children who become ill—are they in emotional pain? We do not know enough about what goes on in children who are ill at the soul level to understand why these challenging experiences occur. However, we do know that children who experience illness not only bring about opportunities for spiritual growth in themselves, but also in the lives of adults around them.

If you are coming solely from the human personality aspect of you, you will of course feel unbearable pain at the suffering of a child. If you are coming from the aspect of the soul, although you will feel pain, you will at the same time be connected to a place of peace inside you. If you come from the aspect of pure spirit, you understand that everyone in the experience is there voluntarily, and that a higher purpose is being worked out in the souls involved. You may experience all of these aspects at the same time. Experiencing unbearable pain, such as a transition of life of a loved one, will give you an experience of knowing that pain, no matter the degree, is transmutable and can be healed.

The Wilderness is lengthy in terms of time—it can seem endless. The temptation to end your Wilderness experience before the divinely appointed time will be hard to resist. Why come so far only to turn back now? Is it that you are not truly ready to depend completely on God for survival, for an indefinite period of time?

You many decide to wander for a little while, because you are testing God. You may say, "I will believe and trust in you for x amount of time. However, if you do not manifest the desires of my heart in the timeframe I set, I will not remain here with you in the Wilderness." But this is not the way this stage of development works. Your time in the Wilderness is the time you need for your consciousness to be raised to a level high enough to move you into the next stage of spiritual development.

If you leave the Wilderness too soon, it is because there is something in your consciousness you are not willing or ready to release. Maybe it is surrendering complete control of your life to a higher power. Maybe it is the notion of service. After the Wilderness phase, you will be called upon to serve your spirit and the spirit of others. If you still have a strong need or desire to serve your ego at this point in the journey, you will leave the Wilderness and serve your ego once more. As the Bible says, a man cannot have two masters—we all know what happens when he does.

Those of you who leave the Wilderness stage of development early: do not fool yourselves. Justifications and rationalizations of how you can still serve your spirit are just that. Anything other than complete surrender of the ego to spirit is you refusing to let go of control of your life. This delay in your spiritual progress is not disastrous, because you can resume your soul's journey in the Wilderness whenever you are ready. But you will reenter the Wilderness where you left off. Whatever you were unable to give up before, you will now have to.

Some people experience the Wilderness stage during one continuous period of time. Others experience it in spans of time that they stretch out over decades or their entire lifetime. They do this until they are ready to complete the work necessary to progress spiritually. Either way—continuous or intermittent progression—will get you to the next stage of development. How fast you want to get there is up to you. God has no preference, but the longer you delay continuing the journey, the longer you will feel empty.

Emptiness comes from a place within you that longs to be filled by spirit. Human beings feel empty almost all of the time, leading to a range of emotions such as: loneliness, boredom, apathy, pain, uneasiness, dissatisfaction, restlessness, resentment, and anger. Why do we experience emptiness? The space that is empty within us has been left so deliberately, so we will seek to fill it. People choose to fill their feelings of emptiness outside of themselves in a plethora of negative ways. But emptiness can only be filled from within. The emptiness inside us has been left as a reminder to awaken to who we really are. Nothing but spirit can fill your emptiness; anything else you attempt to fill it with is a false substitute. How can spirit fill your emptiness?

Emptiness means being devoid of substance. Emptiness is the antithesis of fullness or completeness. One is empty as opposed to being filled. Empty space creates a void; something must exist inside for it to have meaning. In relation to emptiness there is something called fullness; without one state the other would not exist. Both serve a purpose that is vital. Space serves as a way to identify what the *lack* of space feels like. In

Filling the Empty Space

other words, you cannot know fullness or wholeness if you did not first experience emptiness.

You remain empty because you do not allow yourself to become filled with your own spirit. Once again, nothing else can fill you except your spirit. Your spirit is the aspect of you expressing as God: it is your divine self. If you invite it in to fill you, it will: you will be empty no more. When this happens, do not be surprised at how your thinking and behavior will change. You will no longer be dependent on others, or outer things, to fill you. Being filled with spirit takes away the desperation that drives people to pursue outer things and people as a way to find fulfillment. Diligently connect with your spirit on a regular basis, and you will always have the experience of feeling filled.

How does this work? When you arise in the morning and before you go to sleep at night, fill yourself with spirit through meditation. The form or type of meditation is not important. What *is* important is that you fill yourself with spirit when you first awake, before you start your day. You may also choose to do so when your day ends, before you start your slumber. Meditation is one of the surest ways to fill your spirit. No more than 45 minutes of meditation at one sitting is needed for the average person.

Another way to facilitate your filling up with spirit is breathing correctly. Most people do not breathe correctly—they breathe through their mouths, or in a manner inconsistent with harmony. When you breathe, allow yourself to be consciously aware of the sensation of breath expanding in you, then contracting out of you, until this becomes a normal practice. As you inflate, you breathe in spirit; as you exhale, air or stagnant energy escapes through your nose. Each subsequent breath should be deeper than the last, releasing even more used energy back into the atmosphere. When you cultivate a practice of breathing consciously, this enables your mind to become calm. When your breath is released it creates a space within you, which is now ready to be filled with fresh energy emerging from your spirit.

If you are not consciously tuned into this process when it occurs, you will miss the marvel of the experience. Each time you breathe, old used energy is released into the atmosphere, leaving a space for new energy to surge within you, filling you with spirit. Thus, the process of infusing yourself with spirit is constantly taking place—hence the term "inspiration." What is missing is your awareness of it.

The largest obstruction to your being filled with your spirit is the condition of your mind. If there is no space between thoughts that bombard you every second, how can spirit fill you? It cannot. Spirit needs a space or vacuum before it can fill you. There is no space in never-ceasing thoughts for spirit to come through. If you want to be more aware of your spirit, empty the thoughts in your head more thoroughly. The empty space you create will beckon spirit in.

Your spirit is the energy you are made of; it encompasses and surrounds your body that dwells inside of it. When you are empty of thoughts, you become aware of this encompassing energy. Your awareness will act as the conduit to your fulfillment. When you are aware of your spirit, you become aware of the real you. Awareness is essential because when your mind is focused on spirit, it is not focused on anything else. Thus, only spirit exists for you in the present, bringing fulfillment in its wake. Fulfillment is the experience of knowing yourself as spirit. You cannot be fulfilled by knowing yourself as anything else other than your true state of being.

After you have been filled with your spirit, your consciousness becomes a holy space—holy ground, so to speak. It is holy in the sense that the energy of spirit brings holiness or wholeness to your emptiness. When you are no longer empty and you feel whole, you can experience yourself as holy. Holiness is spirit experiencing the whole of itself. Being filled with spirit brings holiness to the space being filled, and thus creates an experience of wholeness. The experience of wholeness brings about the awareness of oneself as divine. So emptiness leads to fulfillment, which leads to holiness, which ends in divinity.

Divinity is the fourth aspect of you: you experiencing yourself as God. The first aspect of you, as a human personality, is the one experiencing the emptiness. The second aspect of you, as a soul, serves as observer to the empty feeling which another part of you is experiencing. A space has now been created in your awareness: the observer and the "experiencer" are not one and the same, and they are not having the same experience. Your spirit, the third aspect of you, fills your empty space with itself. Thus, the empty space in you is made whole, or holy. After all your empty spaces are made holy, you experience the whole of yourself as God.

All of this work does not take place in the Wilderness stage of development. In this stage you are simply asked to become aware that two of you exist: the one experiencing and the one observing. This creates a chasm in your thought system, providing you with a decision about whom you wish to identify with: the part of you that feels empty, or the spirit that fills you.

Fulfillment is an ongoing process, but the process originates in the Wilderness. When you have been filled to a certain level, it is time to leave the Wilderness stage. Remaining still any longer will not serve your spiritual development; it is now time to move to higher ground. You will be led to work in service to your awakened spirit.

The vocation to which you will be called involves work that serves the spirit of others as well as your own. If you are in the Wilderness in the area of a relationship with yourself, you will be called to serve the highest part of you by always coming from a place of self-love. If it is in your home life, you will be inspired to create a physical space that reflects your spirit. If it is in the area of socialization, you may seek out new friends and associates in order to align yourself with people who vibrate at the same energy level as you. If it is in the area of money, you will adopt a consciousness for true prosperity, knowing that its source is God.

If you remain aware, watchful for seeds of opportunity being sent your way, you will be led by spirit on what action to take. Do not doubt those seeds when you become aware of them. The Wilderness is a searching phase. You begin to search for signs—indicators showing which direction you should go. You will be sent these signs through various means.

You might question why you have to search at all. Why can you not be told directly where to go and what to do, every step of the way? If it were easy to know how to proceed, you would miss out on valuable and important opportunities for growth. The very act of searching tunes you into the divine like never before. You will become conditioned to receiving spiritual guidance by waiting on signs telling you how to proceed. This conditioning eliminates your need to look first for external manifestations to occur before you can believe. This is the ego's version of faith.

The work of tuning in for spiritual guidance is new; at first you will be given infant steps to take, before you can walk and then run in truth. Your first step is becoming aware of the divine messages that are constantly sent your way. Awareness is step one. Spirit interacts in the world in every moment: what is missing is your conscious awareness of this fact. After you become aware, you can use the knowledge that spirit imparts to aid you in creating your life.

The signs sent by spirit may look like random coincidences. Do not believe in randomness. You were not created randomly, so why would you believe that anything random exists? Every opportunity that spirit sent and you missed was an event you perceived as random. When you capitalize on perceived random events, you will learn that they are signs from God. Your belief that you are not being led keeps you from recognizing that you are *always* being led.

Filling the Empty Space

Coincidences come to challenge your theory of randomness. After you are sent a sign, take it seriously: remain on constant alert for more. Know that more will be sent if you stay aware. If you follow enough signs, you will reach your destination. Your destination is the place where your spirit leads you, a place that God has in store specifically for you: Your Promised Land.

The good thing about the Wilderness stage is that you will become tired of it. This means that, when you are guided to enter the Jordan River stage, you will not be concerned about the nature or prestige of the work you are initially asked to do. When you are first led out of the Wilderness, you will be placed in a starting or entry-level position in work of a service nature. It does not matter the level of worldly achievement you obtained in Egypt: your old self died in the Wilderness, and in the Jordan River you start anew as spirit. You must humbly and gratefully accept how you are asked to serve.

Although your new position may barely sustain you financially, know that you have been led there for a reason. If you embrace this new experience in gratitude and joy, it will embrace you in return. How long you will stay at the entry level is solely up to you. If you no longer identify with what was, and resist making judgments about where you now are, then you will move quickly up the service ladder. Those who feel gratitude will rise quickly in responsibility, and they will feel content with their humble work. Those who grumble will stay at an elementary stage longer, because they have not yet accepted the joy of providing service in any capacity.

This is a temporary stop—a joyful time. You are back working in the world, this time in service to spirit. The spiritual work to be done in the Jordan River will bring in its wake a host of challenges sufficient unto itself.

118

How are you resisting the spiritual stage of development in which you find yourself?

15

Challenging Your Fears

A NEW SELF, WITH NO history of leadership to bind us to the past, is what we need to reach the Promised Land. Our Moses consciousness led us out of Egypt. It then carried us through the Red Sea and guided us through the Wilderness. But the time has come for it to depart. If our Moses consciousness does not depart after the Wilderness stage, a new leader of our consciousness cannot come forth to lead the new generation of thoughts we acquired in the Wilderness.

It is time for your Joshua Consciousness to awaken within you, to assume leadership of your thoughts. Joshua is the consciousness that represents your new self which is aware of you as a spiritual being. The change in leadership occurs at the end of the Wilderness stage, when you cease identifying with yourself as a human personality. When you start to identify with yourself as spirit, Joshua takes over the reins of leadership.

Your Joshua consciousness has always been with you, assisting Moses. But the conditions in your consciousness are now right for Joshua to take center stage as the primary leader of your new thought system. Your first thought now is of God and of spirit. Joshua represents the awakening or emerging consciousness that calls forth spiritual demonstration.[1]

Joshua has much work to do in the world. This work is done through your spiritual connection with the I Am. There are many lands with false rulers inhabiting territories in your consciousness, and these lands must be liberated for spirit. These rulers must be overthrown, the lands liberated, so that spirit can now claim them for itself. Joshua is the precursor to the fully developed Christ Consciousness that will become the ultimate leader of your thought system.

Your Caleb consciousness will be the only other thought system that accompanies you to the Promised Land. Caleb represents a spirit of boldness and fearlessness within you. It also signifies "spiritual faith and enthusiasm."[2] You are being asked to step out boldly on faith, when you enter the Jordan River. It is there, in the Jordan River, that you will begin the work of serving spirit in the world. Wherever God leads, you must go without delay.

The Promised Land will seem beyond your reach when you are in the Jordan River. Although you are besieged with fear, you must nevertheless pass through these tumultuous tides. Your protection is the faith you have developed in a God who has provided so well for you in the Wilderness. You have an initial period of internal struggle with how and when God's promises will manifest. You must surrender all lingering doubts and fears. You must do the work given to you by spirit. When you have done your part, and you can go no further without divine assistance, God will intervene with a miracle.

Challenging Your Fears

I have often wondered why God does not come when we want him, but just in the nick of time. I used to blame God; now I realize that we are the cause of the delay. A second before he delivers a miracle, we are still not receptive enough to its arrival in our consciousness. It is not God who delays—*we* are the delay. Our fears delay miracles from manifesting. Fear paralyzes us—so much so that our blessings are held in suspended animation, and are slow in coming. When your miracle comes, this will be just the beginning of the work you have to do.

The Jordan River is the time in your development where you will pay your spiritual dues in the world, so to speak. You will never work as hard in the world as when you are in the Jordan River phase. All the rest and solitude you amassed in the Wilderness allowed you to store up a high degree of energy that will now be exerted fully in the Jordan River. You will not be allowed to rest or stay still for very long. If you did not rest as much as you did in the Wilderness, you would not be prepared to cross the Jordan River.

When you are in the Jordan River, you doubt you can ever make it across. The Promised Land seems so far away that you cannot even imagine stepping a foot onto it. In the Jordan River phase, you are called to surpass the perceived limits of your capabilities in the areas of intelligence, competence, and perseverance in the face of insurmountable obstacles. You will be challenged like never before, and you must rise to the occasion. You will not remember what it is like to sleep for more than a few hours at a time. You will barely have time to be still; every moment of your day will be filled with outer work.

The Jordan is a busy stage. It lasts for about a year and a half. At the end of the Jordan stage, after being so thoroughly challenged, a new, more confident self emerges. You know that if you can make it through the trials of the Jordan River, you can make it through anything in life.

What does the Jordan River stage of spiritual development look like? One indicator is that you are actively engaged in the world, doing something that seems larger than your ability to succeed. Your work is extremely challenging, and you are constantly being bombarded with the enormity of the situation. In the Jordan you must step out on your faith and live it daily. There are no safety nets in the Jordan River. Every day you are called to take some action, and to succeed by faith in God alone. You are met with intense outer resistance attempting to prevent your success. You must succeed anyway, and learn to transcend all limits that seek to prohibit your spiritual progression.

When you are in the Jordan River you will be challenged to take a stand and hold your ground. You are no longer a victim of circumstances, and you cannot be pushed around. You are where you are in your life quite purposefully, and you cannot be moved by anyone or anything. In the Jordan River you find your inner strength; you use it as a shield and a defense mechanism when necessary. If your faith is steadfast despite frequent challenges, you will be victorious in every battle that you face. You become a spiritual warrior in the Jordan River phase. Each day you fight to carry on and to do what is asked of you. Nothing will get you through the Jordan other than complete dependence on, and unyielding faith in, God. The Jordan River is not for the weak of heart: only the spiritually strong can survive it.

The Jordan River stage represents the time when all the weeds must be pulled out of your consciousness, by their roots. These weeds are doubts about yourself that still plague you. There are also weeds of fears that paralyze you. It is time to become a gardener: to unearth the overgrown weeds that have run amok in your consciousness for far too long. All of these weeds must be eradicated from your consciousness. This will be done in the Jordan River stage.

In the Jordan, battles are waging on every front: at home, at school, at work, in your relationships, and inside of you. There is no respite. You must find a way to overcome—simultaneously, on every front—the obstacles and challenges that face you. They must be defeated. Although these battles are staged mainly on an outer front, the key to victory is eradicating the weeds that are overgrown in your consciousness.

In the Jordan you will be called to perform Herculean tasks. If you refuse to give up, you will successfully accomplish these tasks. You will experience minor defeats in the Jordan. They are merely stepping-stones on the way, preparing you for your final victory. Although challenging, you will appreciate the Jordan River stage because you will feel lucky and honored that your life has a spiritual purpose. You will be given divine assistance in the Jordan, but you must do your part by asking for it often: you do not receive what you do not ask for.

When Joshua led his people through the Jordan River, which parted for them to cross over, he called forth 12 priests, one representing each tribe of Israel, to bring forward 12 pillars of stone. The pillars were to be taken from the center of the Jordan River and placed in the new land, which had been promised to them by God as testimony to the miracle they had witnessed when the Jordan River parted.[3]

The 12 pillars of stones represent your 12 spiritual facilities that must accompany you into the Promised Land. Your 12 spiritual facilities, as defined by Charles Fillmore, Co-founder of the Unity School of Christianity, are: "faith, strength, wisdom, love, power, imagination, understanding, will, order, zeal, renunciation and life."[4] You can learn more about these spiritual facilities in Fillmore's book, *The Twelve Powers*.[5]

Each of these 12 faculties must be strengthened within you. According to Fillmore, each faculty relates to a specific Apostle and represents a specific attribute in need of development in a certain order in your consciousness. Jesus called to him each Apostle in the order in which you must develop the associated attribute in your consciousness. In the Jordan River, you will be called upon to use and develop each of these facilities. If these faculties are not strengthened, they will continue to wreak havoc in your consciousness and, as a result, your life.

During the Jordan phase of spiritual development, you will be called upon to develop these 12 facilities within you in specific ways. You will be called upon to have faith in an unseen promised future. You will be asked to have faith that God is always with you, working through you. You will be asked to exercise incredible strength, inwardly and outwardly. You will have to develop wisdom and good judgment when dealing with others in the world. Loving yourself and developing good self-esteem become mandatory. You will be asked to gain access to the source of spiritual power within you, so that you can use it. Envisioning yourself (ahead of time) in the Promised Land and believing that a victorious outcome is inevitable will be required of you. You must learn to understand the nature of spirit, how it works and how it manifests itself in the world. The will of the ego must be surrendered in the Jordan.

Although you will feel as if you are fighting for your very existence, there will be a divine order to the challenges that surround you. You will be zealous in the pursuit of spiritual victories. You will renounce fear and self-doubt about yourself and your life. Your final challenge will be transcending the trials and tribulations in your life that are sent your way in order for you to evolve spiritually.

The purpose of strengthening each faculty is for you to develop into a whole or complete being—whole in the sense that each spiritual power has been "quickened" in your consciousness. If you are lacking basic mastery in any of these areas, you will have to work on improving that specific faculty. The call to wholeness is not based on the assumption that you are incomplete. Instead, it is based on the knowledge that, for you to achieve self-awareness as a whole and spiritual being, you must first fully develop the "12 spiritual faculties of man" as defined by Fillmore.

Going through the Jordan is like going through a maze: you do not know where your next step will lead you. You reach a series of dead-ends on this path, leading you back to start anew until you find your way. It is

Challenging Your Fears

a long journey, and you must not give up hope of ever reaching the end. When you are no longer focusing on the end, you will reach it, quickly enough.

You will have to go through the Jordan River during one continuous time period. This differs from the Wilderness stage, which one can leave and revisit again when ready. You do not have the option of leaving when you are in the Jordan River—you have come too far to turn back. There is no time to linger in the Jordan River: stay too long and you will drown in the turbulent tides of your fears. Being required to do difficult things in a short period of time is part of the challenge of this stage of development.

Focus, determination, and persistence are what you need in the Jordan. You will learn that the most effective way of overcoming any seemingly impossible obstacle is to take it in small pieces, one step at a time. Putting effort forward each day in achieving your goals is how you take the necessary steps. Working at a steady pace will eventually lead you to accomplishing your spiritual goals. The lessons you learn as a result of your experiences in the Jordan River help train your inner consciousness in the ways of spirit. A key lesson learned in the Jordan River stage is how to live daily in the now.

When you are near the end of crossing the Jordan River, you will realize an inner state of calmness. All your fears, doubts, and concerns are eradicated. This is because you have gone through them, and overcome them in consciousness. What is left in their wake is peace and calm. You will also feel mentally and physically fatigued after your long voyage through this river, but you will have a brief respite before entering the Promised Land.

You will never forget your Jordan River experiences. The 12 powers that you strengthened within its shores have brought you to an awakened awareness of yourself as a whole spiritual being. In the next stage of spiritual development, the Promised Land, you will be called on to demonstrate your mastery of each of the 12 faculties you strengthened in the Jordan River.

COMPASS

What is it that you most desire to manifest?

16

The Land of Milk and Honey

YOUR JOSHUA CONSCIOUSNESS LED YOU through the Jordan River, and now it leads you into the Promised Land. There you will be met by a host of 31 kings, or adverse thought systems, that still reign supreme in your consciousness. Each king must be defeated, and his lands and inhabitants destroyed. Holding onto the thought patterns and beliefs of any of these kings will erode your spiritual power. All thoughts adverse to spirit must be eradicated in consciousness in the Promised Land.

In the Promised Land you are certain that God will take care of you. This is because, being recently out of the Wilderness and the Jordan River stages of spiritual development, you have learned how to depend on God, and have developed a high degree of faith in him. However, in the early stages of the Promised Land the doubts you will have are about you. You are still a bit dazed from your travels; you need an initial period of adjustment before you will be ready to master this new land.

Others may use the time of your adjustment to test you. When you are engaged in outer conflicts over your worth, realize that these outer battles serve as an indicator that there are areas within you still in need of healing. It is counterproductive to focus on outer conflicts. Your main focus must be on challenging and healing the adverse thoughts within you that are drawing forth these outer attacks.

The low vibration of some adverse thoughts, still lingering in your consciousness, is what attracts the outer attacks you receive at this time. Those people whose energy matches the frequency of your lingering fears will be your adversaries. "As man consciously masters erroneous ideas, which suggest themselves from the external, he masters like ideas in consciousness, which have been the attracting magnet that drew the external experiences to him; he clarifies his heart of the adverse thought until he comes to dwell in the poise and mastery of the Christ self, being master of ideas and their manifestation."[1]

Take responsibility for what is yours to work on, and give to others what is theirs. Never believe somebody else's negative opinion about you; they merely reflect your fears. The only valid opinion to believe about you is the one that God holds. Do not even believe your own opinions about yourself. Adopt God's view of you, and use it to form a higher sense of your worth in consciousness.

Do not perceive adversaries as enemies, but as teachers who come to point out the specific areas in your psyche in need of developing spiritually. No one at this point can truly harm you or prevent your good from manifesting. They can only attack and irritate you—that is, until you eradicate the beacon that your adverse beliefs about yourself are sending out to others. Outer attacks will prove futile in the long run. The key to victory is not to focus on outer attacks, but to instead turn your focus inward to determine what inside you still needs development. Once you evolve in these areas, the outer attacks on you will dissipate.

At times when it may be necessary to fight back in order to defend yourself, by all means do so—to the best of your ability. That is, until you evolve past the need to do so. But do not attack anyone first. As it says in *A Course in Miracles*, "The dreary, hopeless thought that you can make attacks on others and escape yourself has nailed you to the cross."[2] Call on the Holy Spirit for help when being attacked, or when you are contemplating attacking others.

You must authentically operate from the place where you are in consciousness. There are times when you will decide to challenge other people's right to judge and criticize you. Sometimes doing nothing when attacked is the worse thing that one can do: it merely encourages others to prolong their attacks. You will have to discern when it is appropriate to take some outer action. When you do so, make sure that you do not attack others—not even in your thoughts. Judging others is indicative of a lower level of consciousness. The goal must be to strive always for the highest possible conscious awareness of spirit. When at times we fall short of doing this, we must gently remind ourselves that although we may have missed the mark, our inherent nature is still one of spirit, which is holy.

Bless your adversaries. You have to authentically get to a place where attacks can no longer budge you from where you are in consciousness. This occurs when nothing can disturb the peaceful inner state that you cultivate. All adversaries or adverse thoughts will eventually fall by the wayside. Recognize that others are going through their own stages of spiritual development. Holding onto resentment towards them will keep you trapped in the same lower resonance of consciousness that is seeking to attack you. The most effective form of revenge is success, which can be defined as remaining at a place of peace within you despite outer attacks. Allow attacks to your peace to become background chatter that you can barely hear.

What is the Promised Land? It depends on what life area you are focusing on. In the area of work, the Promised Land is the place where you fulfill your spiritual calling to serve. You will be given elementary tasks to do initially. When you are called to serve in an even higher capacity, your first response will be one of fear. You will feel as if you are being called to do something that is too high in vision and scope for you. You will resist, delay, and deny your spiritual gifts even in the Promised Land.

After having no choice left but to face your fears, you will come to realize that if you do not use your God-given spiritual gifts, you will lose them. Your opportunity to experience yourself as divine will go with them. How you handle, in consciousness, both the internal and external challenges you face during this time determines when and how you will proceed spiritually.

The spiritual ability to create does not become dormant over a short period of time; it takes decades before neglect will cause you to begin to lose this ability. If you delay too long in resurrecting it, one day you will realize that you have missed your chance to do so. As Wayne Dyer says, "Don't die with your music still in you."[3] Your fears must be faced, challenged, and overcome. The definition of courage is being scared and doing it anyway. Go shaking, weeping, feeling paralyzed and terrified—but *go*. You must move. If, by procrastinating, you continue to justify your fears that you will use your spiritual gifts sometime in the future, or if you try to work up your courage slowly, or use any other delaying tactic, you will pay the ultimate price. That price will be living an unfulfilled life with the knowledge that it did not have to be this way.

The truth is, you are afraid because you do not think you are good enough, or worthy enough, to be successful. You feel inadequate because you identify with your ego mind, which believes in your imagined frailties. You still erroneously believe that you are the one who will be doing all of the work necessary to be successful. You have not yet accepted that a higher power working through you will be doing the work. Your only job is to be receptive—an empty vessel through which this higher power can work.

You will have to face your fears and thoughts about money. A lot of spiritual people falsely believe that money and spiritual work should not go hand and hand. This belief must be challenged and released: you have not yet learned that money is simply energy. The sponsoring force behind all energy is love, which is also another name for God. How then can love and money not go hand in hand?

You will fear recognition for your work, because you do not want to be singled out for your achievements. You want to hide anonymously behind your creations. Why do you think this is? Could it be because, although you have always imagined yourself on center stage, actually finding yourself there will no longer allow you to deny the truth about yourself? If you continue to deny the truth about yourself and how great you truly are, others will continue to like you—or so you think. You also desire to hide because you are uncomfortable with being visible. Being seen heightens your vulnerabilities. Your ego can also continue to believe that others, who have chosen to use their spiritual gifts, are somehow better than you. Instead of recognizing that we all have an equal amount of potential, it is merely a question of developing it.

Fear is a terrible thing, but as Wayne Dyer said, quoting a proverb, "Fear knocked at the door. Love answered and no one was there."[4] Fear is the antithesis of love. There are two basic states or poles of being: love and fear. Both cannot exist in the same space. So you must choose: which state will you allow yourself to come from? When you are feeling fear, and its offshoots doubt and worry, it is because you have removed yourself from a state of love. A state of love is found in your spirit, not in your mind. Your mind and other people's minds typically project fear onto you. So you must leave your mind empty and allow spirit to fill it. If you are constantly with God in a place of love, you will transcend the feeling of fear.

Your spirit will start to feel restless and unsatisfied with the status quo. God will begin to send you many messages and signs. It will become obvious after a while that it is time to increase your territory. You can think of the Promised Land as having 31 sublevels within in it, through which one must evolve to become the fully developed Christ. After a lengthy stay in the first sublevel of the Promised Land, you will be a bit reluctant to move at first. This is because you will have gotten used to routine, especially that of regular paychecks. But you must not worship mediocrity, or make a god of paychecks. You must be ready to give up all that you have acquired since entering the Promised Land, when you are called to journey anew. When the call to journey comes, you must be ready to answer it in faith.

In truth, if you are honest with yourself, you will admit that you are relieved to be in motion once again. You have outgrown in consciousness your current outer physical environment. Does not some part of you yearn for more adventure? There is nothing more adventurous than living a spiritual life. Fear and doubt will still plague you, but they must be tackled and overcome. The only way you can doubt your future is if you believe that God will not be there. Was God there for you in the Wilderness? Was God there for you in the Jordan River? Are you saying that he has led you this far only to abandon you now? Are you afraid that God will abandon you—or are you afraid that *you* will abandon yourself and God?

The real problem stems from your erroneous belief that you are lacking in worth. You fear that God thinks too highly of you. Do you not think that Moses, Joshua, and Jesus all felt the same way? Could they deny their purpose in life? How then do you think that you can deny yours? You may delay it for a few lifetimes, but you can never deny it indefinitely. If you are a spiritual being (and spirit exists in all beings), if there is only one universal spirit and you are one unique aspect of it, then what is the problem? The problem is that you have not fully accepted who you are in spirit. You toy with the notion, but you have not fully accepted it.

You are the Christ, the son or daughter of God, endowed with the same creative powers of the original Creator. To deny this is to deny the entire journey. Is it not far simpler to pray, "God, I need some help in accepting my divinity. Will you help me to do so?" God will answer your prayer for help.

In the Wilderness, having some doubts was acceptable because you were at an initial stage of spiritual development. However, in the Promised Land, all doubts must be placed aside. If you still doubt, this suggests that a significant amount of fear still exists within you. You must find the origin of this fear and eradicate it. Fear can never serve you—fear serves your ego. Why do you fear? Is it because in your mind, God's promises are too good to be true? Who asked your mind anyway? You are spirit. If God's promises sound too good to be true, it is because you are not aligned properly in consciousness with the I Am. All things are possible through a belief in God who strengthens you.

After completing the first sublevel in the Promised Land, you will be called to surrender all you have accomplished in the territory you now occupy. The Promised Land has now turned into Egypt. You have to leave Egypt once again and evolve through the subsequent stages of spiritual development, concluding in reentrance to the Promised Land at a higher sublevel.

Having to start the journey over again from the beginning may surprise you, since you have already traveled through all the stages of spiritual development necessary to obtain the Promised Land consciousness. In fact you have. However, in order to enlarge your spiritual territory and receive more blessings, your consciousness must evolve even higher. It does this by journeying again through each of the stages of spiritual development: Egypt, the Red Sea, the Wilderness, the Jordan River, and then the next sublevel in the Promised Land.

This may seem frightening to you—starting the journey of the soul over again, after all that you already experienced. Why is it necessary to do this, you might ask? The question is a valid one. The answer may surprise you: you are ready for greatness. The call to move again is an indication that the job given to you has been well done. In truth, you have become stagnant in your spiritual development. You are now easily able to handle the challenges that appear in your life. Your work seems boring to you again, and you feel restless. Your spirit begins to urge you to leave where you are. This sense of urgency growing in you seems familiar.

Think back and ask yourself where you have encountered these feelings before. It was when you were in Egypt, being called by your spirit to originate the journey of your soul. Did you think that spirit was through with you—that you would remain where you were forever? You were where you needed to be for a reason: to evolve in consciousness. You have now grown sufficiently to move to a higher place in consciousness. What occurs in the inner must be manifested in the outer—so your outer circumstances must now match your new inner conditioning. Your "divine discontent," as my former minister used to call it, is summoning you to be moved to higher ground in consciousness.

Still you are apprehensive to begin the journey anew. Let us be clear as to why. You may erroneously believe it is because you will have to give up your steady income, the place you now live in, or you fear that you will go back to a less prosperous state. It is none of these reasons that you delude yourself with. The truth is simple and straightforward: you fear to accept your destiny and your greatness. In truth, you know that you have come too far in consciousness for manifesting anything that you need, including money, to be much of a problem for you. You tell yourself these things in order not to deal with your sponsoring fearful thought. This thought is: I am not worthy enough to fulfill my destiny. As it says in A Course in Miracles, "Your worth is not established by teaching or learning. Your worth is established by God. As long as you dispute this everything you do will be fearful, particularly any situation that lends itself to the belief in superiority and inferiority."[5] Can we then continue to deny that we are worthy?

Who are you in truth? Was God somehow wrong about you? Did he go off track when creating you? Did God envision a destiny too large for you to fulfill? Or does the problem lie in the ego's beliefs about you? It is time to accept your greatness. The world is in need of greatness; insisting that you are inadequate is what you need to surrender in order to accept God's vision for your life.

Is it frightening to begin anew the journey of the soul in any life area? Whether or not it is depends on how you perceive it. Is it scary to visit old and familiar places within yourself? It may be, if you were not traveling these familiar lands as a master, but you are. You have now become the master of your soul. What does this mean? It means that you have mastered enough of yourself that your spirit is in full control of you. Do not be frightened about the journey that you will undertake: you will undertake it as a master. A master who knows what is coming and is prepared in consciousness to transcend it. Tremble no more. Destiny: it awaits you.

COMPASS

Why do you care about others' opinions of you?

17

Adverse Thinking

I N TRUTH, YOU ARE GREAT. Now that the opportunity has come for you to move to higher ground in consciousness, do not bemoan the work to be done—welcome it. This work is a gift sent to answer your spirit's call for greatness. If you do not know or believe this, align yourself with divine mind to experience the truth of who you really are. Your spirit has a higher vision for your life. It remembers how it feels to soar without any limitations. You have brought about the challenges you now face in your life in order to usher in change.

There is a part of you that misses miracles. When is the last time you were able to manifest one? Another part of you misses the excitement of not knowing what would come next in life, and secretly yearns to live life again as an adventure instead of a predictable routine. Yet an even greater part of you craves to be and experience so much more in life. Your spirit is aware of all of this. Did you think that these feelings did not matter, or that the yearnings of your soul could be ignored indefinitely?

Aligning your mind with God is what is needed at the start of the journey. The main source of misery for most people is a belief in the thoughts they hold in their mind. Those thoughts can in turn bring about emotions of fear and doubt. The problem with fear and doubt is that they are energies that cannot easily be penetrated; they are dense in matter and occupy too much space in your consciousness. If you can control the effect that these two energies have on you, you can overcome them.

The first thing you need to do to combat negative fearful energy is say to yourself, "I have a hard time accepting the good that God has for me. Since I do not know the future, I will choose to believe God's version of it." When you choose to believe your own version of how it will turn out, you allow in fear and doubt. *Be willing not to know*: the doubt-and-fear-filled thoughts you have about your future may be wrong. Are you at least willing to accept this?

Choose to align with your spirit, knowing that the highest possible outcome will occur. All that is needed is an opening in your mind—parted waters—where you allow the spirit of God to come in and raise you above the troubling waves of fearful thoughts and doubts. If you invite God in, he will come in and transport you in consciousness to a higher level of awareness. Your fears cannot reach you here; they are too low in energy, and thus cannot tune into the higher frequency.

How do you invite God in? With a simple prayer where you tell God that you need his help. God will not delay in coming to your aid if you first get yourself out of the way. However, when you are delivered to a higher place in consciousness, you cannot allow yourself to be brought lower in consciousness once again by thoughts that are contrary to your good.

If you do not learn to control your mind and its adverse thinking when you are in the Promised Land, you will not meet with much success. You must learn how to un-think. It is a fallacy that the more you think, the smarter you are. In fact, the opposite is quite true. The more you are mentally silent, the more inspiration and knowledge can come through you. Wisdom is following the guidance given from a higher place within you.

Thinking laboriously about anything will never help you—in fact it often defeats you. Most battles are fought and lost in the thinking process. Your dreams never have an opportunity to reach the light of day. When you are divinely inspired or led to do anything, you do not act right away. Instead, you waste critical time thinking and mulling things over first. This is as far as most people get: it takes a lot of energy to move after a lifetime of adverse thinking.

Why it is necessary for you to constantly think about your actions first, before taking action? It may be because you cannot just accept truth at its most basic level. If a divinely inspired idea comes to you, give it no thought. Whether or not you agree with it, do not think about it. Merely allow yourself to *be* with it. This is all that is needed. Fear and doubt originate from over-thinking. It is often taught in spiritual circles to mentally picture a positive outcome before it manifests. This is because it allows you to accept your blessings in consciousness on some level ahead of time. However, you cannot hold a positive picture in your mind without also picturing a negative one. So it is better to remain empty—devoid of any pictures or thoughts in your mind at all.

You have been conditioned since birth to fear, doubt, and question, when instead you should have been taught to listen, observe, be, and know. If you do not believe that you are worthy and deserving of your highest good, you will never receive it. Not because you are being punished: the reason is that your mind will attempt to self-sabotage all of your good and prevent it from occurring. All you will receive is a small amount of good that is able to trickle through the cracks in the wall of fear that your ego has erected.

Although this good is nominal, it is enough for most people on Earth. Why is this? Those who receive their highest good know that they are worthy of it on some level. If they do not believe they are worthy, they at least believe that good is possible, and ask why they should not receive it. At the very least, they believe that they are at least as good as anybody else.

The issue of good and worth must be dealt with and resolved once and for all if you are going to proceed successfully in the Promised Land. If it is so easy for you to believe in fearful things, can you not train yourself to just as easily believe in loving and authentic things? Whether or not you are aware of it, spirit is here to support you. It is far easier for it to support you than to impede you. If you do not feel supported, it is because you create a barrier to help by thinking thoughts adverse to your good.

I cannot stress enough how important it is for you to learn to control your thoughts. Do so now, before your potential good is thwarted. Challenge every thought held in your mind, even if it is not overtly negative. Saying positive affirmations will serve you in the short term. But evolving beings do not need to *think* about their good one way or another: they *know* it at the highest level of their being.

This is the level of consciousness needed for manifestation to occur in your reality. Do not mull something over mentally. Instead, through an absence of thoughts, remain focused and rise to the vibration of the good you are attempting to manifest. This will bring about an experience of knowingness that will expedite manifestation.

The function of the mind is not to debate or analyze. The mind is meant to be an instrument where divinely inspired guidance and inspiration can be received. It is a tool of spirit. When you receive a divine revelation or inspiration, remain mentally still. Accept that you have received a divine message, but do not allow yourself to think it over: merely be with it. You can ask clarifying questions at the time when you are receiving the inspiration. But after you have been given your answers, question no more. If something changes, you will be told or led to discover it. The mind was never intended to be a fully operating entity, separate from and in conflict with the spirit. The proper alignment of the mind is under the control of spirit.

You are sad, bored, lonely, unhappy, fearful, doubtful, and poor because you think you are. You could not truly be anything of these things if you were not first thinking them into existence. Prosperity, harmony, unity, and good are all natural states of being. Because these are natural states, anything contrary to them is unnatural. Most human beings live unnaturally. Is this a surprise to anyone? What is surprising is that you allow yourself to remain indefinitely in unnatural states, with no end in sight.

The spirit knows the truth about itself and is never in any place other than love. The question is, where are *you*? You are not with your spirit. If you were, you could not be experiencing anything but love and its offshoots: peace and joy. Your mind is making you ill by bombarding you with thoughts of dissatisfaction with your life. It lulls you into believing that, by constantly thinking and mulling over feelings of unhappiness, this very act will make things get better. You will not feel any better until you stop thinking. When you allow yourself a break in forming thoughts, you start to feel better. Have you ever noticed this?

Why is it that human beings must have mental conversations about most everything with themselves? They do so before things happen, while they are happening, and after they occur. Why is all this mental chatter necessary? How many thoughts do you have in one day? Are most of them necessary? Are any? Well, maybe a small percentage. If you do not rise above the level of the mind, you will have difficulty receiving your good. The ideal state of your mind should be like a river: that is, calm, flowing, and quiet. You must allow your thoughts to flow through your mind like currents, never lingering for very long. Do not take any notice of thoughts as they pass through and out of your mind. Do not use this analogy to create a *picture* of water in your mind; emulate the *essence* of water.

When your mind is still, if you are not doing any activity you might fall asleep. This is because the mind associates stillness with an indication that it is time to go to sleep. Because this is the only time that the mind receives any relief from your thoughts, it might help to keep your eyes open when you are being mentally still. Your mind will eventually learn that quietness is not a trigger for sleep.

When your mind is still, you tune into your spirit. The peace of your spirit will at first also lull you to sleep. The body thinks if you are with your spirit, then it must be rest time. This can be overcome by learning to quiet your mind while performing any activity. You can listen to music, watch television, cook, exercise, and allow your mind to remain in quiet unison with these activities. There will be one part of you involved in some action, while mentally you remain still. After you master quieting the mind in this way, then try mental stillness without performing any activity. However, you should do this when you are sitting up, so that you do not fall asleep. You will eventually master the art of quieting and stilling the mind under all conditions. If you do not practice transcending your mind, you will never become proficient at it.

Quieting the mind is only a means to get you somewhere. After the mind is quiet, you will be able to reach your spirit more easily. The energy that you free up by quieting your mind becomes energy that can be used in service to your spirit. Most of your self-sabotaging behavior is a direct result of the condition of your mind. The challenges that are sent to you in life often come by way of the mind. Your mind is not a bad thing—in fact it is quite useful. It is even more useful when used in the way that it was intended. If you diligently work on elevating your mind to a higher place of consciousness on a consistent basis, you will become aware of yourself as a spiritual being. Constant vigilance is necessary; as soon as you slack off on stilling the mind, your thoughts will return to their previous uncontrolled state.

When you liberate yourself from identification with the mind, you will heal. The only way for you to heal is through your spirit, which comes to liberate you from the constraints of your mind. As your mind is still, your perception and awareness become keener. You will become more vividly aware of the colors of ordinary objects, which will seem more vibrant. That is because coming from a place of spirit infuses you with more energy, thus increasing your perception. When you come from a place of spirit, you often feel love and joy for no reason. You feel contentment.

When you call more of your spirit into being, you will have more energy to use. This energy will enable you to do miraculous things, because your consciousness will now have been fully awakened to its divinity. Is it necessary to produce astounding miracles? Not really—it depends on your purpose on Earth. The miracles you call forward are generally routine and involve your everyday life. What is a miracle, other than faith in a perceived outcome before it happens, fueled with the energy of love?

A miracle worker is one who has awakened to the divinity within, and is no longer ruled by the mind or body, but by spirit. When you are working in the energy of spirit, miracles will not seem quite as astonishing to you. A miracle is your confirmation that you are on the right track; it encourages you to delve further into raising your consciousness. When you reach the Christ Consciousness stage of spiritual development, it will become possible to see past matter in its illusory three-dimensional form. Instead, you see matter as infinite energy, which can be formed and shaped into any desired form. Jesus' miracles grew in nature as his realization of himself as the Christ grew.

The purpose of developing your consciousness to the level of Christ is not to perform miracles. When you reach a certain stage of consciousness, being able to perform miracles will occur naturally, as a byproduct of the journey. But that is not the goal. The goal is for you to be in service to humanity. By the time you reach this stage of development, you will be done with being of service solely to yourself and your own spiritual development. Helping others is also a way of serving yourself because we are all one in consciousness. You will continue to evolve, but now you will evolve through helping others.

Miracle workers are those who use their energy of love in a tangible way when working in the world. These people are on Earth purely to serve humanity. Jesus Christ was one such person, the Buddha another—as were Mother Teresa, and Paramahansa Yogananda, along with many others in every major religion. These individuals have reached a stage of enlightenment where they have realized their divinity.

Miracle workers serve in two basic ways: by uplifting humanity through their individual level of consciousness, and by serving others in the world. Jesus came to Earth not only to raise the consciousness of the world; he also came to provide the means for people to have a viable relationship with the Creator. Also, he came to eradicate the belief that life ends after physical death. The mission of the Buddha was different. His task in part was to demonstrate that one could attain "full awakening" and liberation from suffering while on Earth.

There are still miracle workers on the Earth today, both young and old. They are not always recognized. Everyone on Earth has the potential to become a miracle worker. This position is open to all who are willing to take the journey of the soul, and to heed the call of spirit. After you reach the Promised Land, you will be asked to answer the call, joining those who came before you in uplifting humanity through imparting love and spiritual wisdom to the world.

The Promised Land has approximately 31 sublevels before you reach the level of the fully developed Christ. These sublevels can also be thought of as settlements in your consciousness, which must be liberated for the use of spirit. Your spirit must become ruler over these lands that once were ruled by your ego. To describe each sublevel would not be beneficial; some might apply to you where others might not. It is best left for you to forge through these new lands yourself.

The important thing to remember is that after completing each sublevel in the Promised Land, you become more evolved in consciousness. Thus, life's trials will have less of an impact on you. Your spirit will let you know when you have completed the required work in each sublevel, and when it is time to advance to higher ground. You will spend the rest of your life doing this work. When will the work of striving to reach the Christ Consciousness stage of spiritual development end? This is not important—mastering each stage of development *is*. Every spiritual leader and miracle worker had to undertake the same journey within to reach the Christ Consciousness stage of spiritual development.

You will not be perfect when you complete all of the sublevels in the Promised Land; Jesus himself was not perfect. This may seem blasphemous to some—but what purpose would Christ serve as a master teacher if he already came in a state of perfection? He came in a near-perfect state and had to overcome life, in order to show you how you too could obtain the Christ level of consciousness. It is not an insult to state the truth. Insisting on Christ being perfect negates the important lessons he came to teach. Jesus taught by example, and gave humanity a blueprint of the stages of spiritual development as a precursor to becoming the fully evolved Christ. Jesus had a complete human experience on Earth before becoming the Christ. Follow in his footsteps and join with him in service to the world.

Everybody is a teacher. What you will teach depends on what you most need to learn. Christ's legacy on Earth is not over—it did not die with his physical body over 2000 years ago. The legacy he left is to enable individuals to express their divinity, and to be more consciously, more fully aware of it.

God is in need of miracle workers, those willing to answer the call of spirit to serve. No two spirits can do the same job in the same exact way; each spirit brings something unique to their experience. Do not ignore your spirit's mission out of fear that you have nothing unique to offer the world. Do not allow this fear-based excuse to prevent you from keeping your divine appointment with God. Whatever you create will be unique because of the very fact that it emanated from you. A place in service awaits you, and only you can fill it perfectly. Many question if they have a divine purpose in life—or if life has any specific purpose at all. Your divine purpose in life is to experience your divinity, and this is more readily done through work of a service nature.

Your divine calling is simple to ascertain, although you make finding it seem like an impossible task. Your divine calling is the thing that you most desire to do, but are too afraid to dare believe that you could really achieve. It is your heart's desire, as Emmet Fox, a great New Thought mystic, called it. It is the yearning that lies in the most sacred place within you. It is the thing that you are afraid to say aloud for fear of getting laughed at. That which seems to you an impossible dream is your divine work in this life. Do you have the courage to pursue it? Life, to your spirit, is not about making a living. It is about creating and experiencing the highest and most fulfilling life possible on Earth, while taking the journey of your soul. Answer the call of spirit and do the unique work only you can do in service to humanity.

What are some of the techniques that you can utilize to quiet your mind and keep fear at bay?

18

Becoming the Christ

WHAT DOES IT MEAN TO be the Christ? There is no job description for becoming the Christ, no set of guidelines for you to follow. Being the Christ means that you have developed your own indwelling spiritual characteristics to their highest potential. How this will look in each individual is unique. Unique is a word that God likes. God has given us many similarities, but the I Am delights in the unique features he has given each of us. Uniqueness is a form of individual expression; we are all unique and yet similar at the same time.

At the Christ Consciousness stage of spiritual development you are aware of yourself as nothing but spirit. Two of you no longer exist in consciousness; one of you has been given up for the other, the lower for the higher. Choose the Christ in you as the identity with which you most identify. For in truth, it is your only identity. The term "the Christ" does not refer to any religious figure; the term is not synonymous with any particular religion. It is used to describe the highest state of spiritual attainment one can acquire, as a result of achieving mastery in spiritual evolution. A Buddhist can reach the Christ stage of spiritual development.

Why would one want to realize the Christ stage of spiritual development? One does not want to—one's *spirit* does. It is inherent in the makeup of spirit to strive for this. To seek while being fully aware, however, is the experience of masters. The masters are those who have obtained, through spiritual development, the consciousness of the Promised Land in each area of their lives. They bring their whole being to the process of evolution. Being a master does not mean you have nothing further to learn; it means you have reached a place where higher-level learning can take place. Everything up until to this point has been preparatory in nature. For masters there can be no higher experience than expressing their divinity fully while on Earth.

Christ was a master; so too was the Buddha, Moses, and many others. We know of many masters, but there are even more of whom we have never heard. I am a master in training and so are you—we are all masters in training. There is no one on this planet who is not a master. We are all masters of *something*. The only question that begs to be answered is—what is he or she a master of? Are you a master of truth and spirit, or have you made the ego and illusions your master? Only you can answer this question for yourself.

To master something means to acquire the highest level of proficiency in a certain area, or in many areas. When you are a master your reaction in every possible scenario becomes constant. You make the highest viable choice. Masters have come to learn that, regardless of the situation, there is always only one choice. They know the answer to the question, "Who are you?" The response is always: "I am love!" When you know who you are, then the only question remaining is, "How would love act?" Thus the equation is made simple: love times anything equals love (love x ? = love). It does not matter what challenges your state of love: you fill in the blank and the product will remain the same. The only product of any action is love; all other results are false. Masters are those who have come to know this.

Masters choose the highest outcome in most circumstances. I say "most" because they too are imperfect. They can miss the mark at times. Mastery and perfection are not one and the same. Mastery is more synonymous with the word "consistency." Masters are consistent in their behavior. They are not erratic and do not respond in ways that conflict or deviate from their spirit; this is due to their level of spiritual development. Mastery is the state we are all working to attain. Mastery is not about perfection: it is about consistently coming from the highest place within you, and knowing that there is only one choice to make. Am I going to express the truth about myself, or do I still need to pretend that I am another? Masters always come from a place of truth.

This is the crossroads where everyone must arrive. At its junction, an arrow points in two different directions. One direction leads inside of you, while the other leads to a place outside of you. It is up to you to choose which path to follow. There is only one authentic choice available: the choice for your spirit. The I Am that I Am can no longer do anything to aid you unless you make this choice. You have come a long way on the journey of the soul, but you can advance no further unless you take the next crucial step. You must begin your life anew as spirit. Even if you are not yet comfortable in this new role, you must choose to act from it anyway. In so doing, you prepare yourself for a new stage of spiritual development, one as the Christ.

What keeps you from becoming the Christ and developing spiritually? The answer is your creation the ego, and its persistent belief in illusions. Illusions can be defined as beliefs created in place of the truth. You have created something in place of the truth in almost every area of your life. Illusions surround you like air, only visible through the eyes of the ego. You live in a made-up and self-created world of illusions because you are not willing to accept the truth about most anything.

To accept the truth means you must give up your own personal truth. When your truth does not match the truth being shown you, you fight to hold onto your own version of truth. This is how illusions are created. Illusions are tools of the weak; those who are weak in spirit cling to illusions for support. Truth is the tool of spirit. Truth is the antithesis of illusion. Illusions are what you have created in place of truth.

You desperately want your illusions—more than you want truth. Your illusions, as you envision them, hold the key to fulfillment of your every wish. Let us look at this more carefully. You have left it up to your ego to decide what you want. Then you allowed it free rein in determining how your desires were to be fulfilled. You painted a mental picture of what this fulfillment should look like. You then surrounded this mental picture with all of your focused energy. This picture, turning out exactly how you imagined, it is what you call happiness or success.

You have created an illusory trap. You first identified some lack; then you came up with a way to fill it. This lack being filled in a specific way, as determined by your ego, is the only alternative you are willing to accept. So let us recap: you identified a lack, you created a way for it to be filled, and then you became attached to it unfolding according to your ego's wishes. Can you see the conflict that you have created in yourself?

You must ask yourself this question: "who is it that first identified any lack in me, and in my life?" Spirit identifies only with wholeness and completeness. It could not have been your spirit, so that leaves only one option: ego. So your ego saw lack, came up with a solution or a plan to fill it, and then refused to give up its attachment to fulfillment according to its wishes. Everything you attempt to create from the place of ego is as untrue as its creator. The ego is the creator of illusions. This may be hard for you to accept, but it is the truth.

The first false assumption your ego made was that a lack of any kind existed in you, or in your life. The main deficiency that most human beings erroneously perceive is a lack of love in their lives. They see love as something they are deficient in, so they create a whole mythology around how to get and keep it. We determine where love is to be found, how it should look, and how we should receive it.

But suppose that your original premise was wrong. Suppose you did not lack love at all: then what? Your whole search for it outside of yourself would be in vain, would it not? "Perish the thought" is probably what is going through your mind. But this is precisely what must be done. You must allow the false belief that you are without love to perish and die. You were not created without love—so how can you now be without the very substance you were created in? You cannot. Everything that is in God is in you. How then can you be without something that can be found within you? You cannot. You can believe that you can be without it, and thus starts the illusion.

The ego cannot tune into that which is in you, because the ego's birth takes place outside of you. It exists solely in the land out there, a place outside of spirit. So how can it look inside of you, a place it has no conception of? It cannot. Your illusions, based on the perspective of your ego, are never questioned or challenged by your soul. You assume that they are true. Then you build your whole life around false illusions that reflect the ego's wants and desires back to you. The ego has created a world of illusions; it is called your life. It is time for you to leave this distorted reality and return to a place of truth and love found inside you.

Let us challenge the biggest weapon in the ego's arsenal: the notion that you lack love. You believe this illusion; thus it causes you to suffer greatly. The presumption is that you are without love, so you go in search of another to love you and fill a supposed place of lack within you. When another does not do this—or cannot for an indefinite period of time—you start to imagine you must be unlovable. You stop loving yourself because you could not get confirmation from another that you are worth loving. So not only do you not love yourself, believe that you are without love and unlovable; you begin to think you are unworthy or undeserving of receiving love because you secretly accept the opinions of others who withhold love from you. They cannot be wrong, you think. You cannot be wrong either, because there is no love in your life, no one to love you.

But you are wrong—tragically wrong.

Let us examine, one at a time, all of these illusions created by the ego. The first one is that you lack love. God did not create you without love—in fact God did not create anything without the spiritual energy of love. To do so would be blasphemous. It would go against the very nature of creation itself to create from other than the essence of what it is, i.e. love. All creation is an expression of self. Because there is no lack of love in the original creative self, there can be no lack of love in its creations. God is love, and he created you in love. Love is found within you, the creation of God. This is absolute truth.

The problem is not that you do not have love; the problem is that you do not know where to *find* it. Like most others on the planet, you assume that love is to be found outside of you. Did it ever cross your mind that what you seek most might be found elsewhere—inside of you? No; human beings do not arrive at this conclusion until they have exhausted all outer efforts to find love. It is only when they have failed miserably in these attempts, and admit defeat, that they become open to the possibility that maybe the very premise that they lack love is false. The root of the problem is that they were looking for love in all the wrong places.

No matter where you are in the never-ending search for external love, heed these liberating words: love is found inside you. You are not without it, nor have you ever been. There is no point in seeking love outside of yourself. What you seek has been found and is waiting to be claimed inside.

We must clarify what it is that we seek. What is love? To most, love is defined as a feeling or sensation of joy, goodness, or wish fulfillment. Few understand what love truly is—it is none of these things. Love is a condition or state of being. Love, in fact, is the authentic state of being of the spirit. Love is the energy that your spirit emits. It is spirit expressing itself. Love is also a place from which you come. It is not something that you can be given, or that you can acquire from a source outside of yourself.

You can be a participant in the experience of someone coming from a state of love found inside when they are with you. But they are not giving you the state from which they are coming. Others may choose to come from a different state, such as anger, when with you. Will you then be without love, because another has chosen to come from a lower state of being when in relationship with you? No: it does not matter what state another comes from—what matters is what state *you* come from. If you are not coming from a place of spirit, you are bereft of authentic love.

The love I am referring to is the love that emanates from your spirit. You can never be without it; you are the source of it. Your spirit is the source of your love. Any time you falsely believe you are without love, return to a place of spirit found within you. Coming from a place in spirit gives you an experience of who you are—in other words, love. That is why experiencing the energizing force of love is so enjoyable: it gives you a relative experience of who you really are. Therefore, coming from a place of love is not a gift that you give another whom you are in relationship with—it is a gift you give *yourself*.

When you express love, you are giving its benefits to yourself. If you consistently choose to come from a place of love, then you will consistently receive it from yourself. But even if you do not choose to come from a place of love, you are still never without it—it is the very energy of which you are made. To reiterate: love is the energy that emanates from your spirit.

If you feel you are without love, ask yourself how much time you spend with your spirit. The extent to which you do determines the depth of your connection to the love within you. The ego was wrong: you did not lack love at all. In fact, it is the true state of your being, so the mission to seek it outside of yourself has become a moot point. Why do you have to seek externally for something that exists within you? Or could it be that you have never taken the time to look first within? Instead you initiated a futile search for it externally.

God never thought you would believe you were without love. God placed love somewhere he was sure that you would look: inside of you. He never thought that you would not look inside first. There is no great mystery surrounding how to acquire love; it was always a state that you could access within yourself. The madcap adventure that most people spend their lives on, searching for love outside of themselves, is disheartening.

The search for love causes so much confusion and misery in the lives of millions, and it is all for naught. The I Am that I Am is saying, "look for love within you. Know it is there that you will find it. I am sorry that your search outside of yourself has been in vain. Stop looking for love, for it is not lost and thus needs not be found. Eradicate the false belief that you are unworthy of love simply because another did not choose to come from a place of spirit when in relationship with you. There is no one who does not have love inside of them. God has put it inside of everyone, with no exceptions. If you are connected to the source of love inside of yourself, do you need another to give love to you?"

Let us challenge the ego's second false belief: that loves emanates or can be received from another. If love is the state of your spirit and you give yourself a relative experience of love by expressing it or coming from it, are you not in fact giving love to yourself? Do you truly get love from another? No.

This is radical thinking for most of you. But love is not something you can receive from another. You share in the experience of another giving love to themselves through their interactions with you. However, you do not receive love directly from another—you are a participant in the process of others giving love to themselves. You are used as a focal point for others to have a relative experience of their spirit as love. In other words, you provide another with opportunities to come from a place of love when with you, thus giving them a relative experience of themselves as being love itself. Love is energy that needs constant expression in order to evolve into higher states.

You can be a participant in the process of people coming from a place of ego as well. The ego has its own counterfeit version of love—it is called fear. Fear masquerades as love according to how the ego defines it. A vast number of people in romantic relationships have many experiences of unfounded fear. They lose sight of what authentic love feels like, and learn to see fear as a normal part of an experience of romantic love.

Only you can give yourself love; no one else can do it for you. Other people can love you, and they can express the state of love within themselves when they are with you. But they cannot give you the state of love that they are coming from. So the search for another to give you love must end. You must come to understand that your role in a relationship is to assist the spirit of another. This is done by allowing the spirit of another to express the energy of love freely and without hindrance with the purpose being their relative experience of it.

Those of you who feel unhappy and miserable because you feel another did not love you understand what is truly going on. Another simply chose not to come from a place of spirit within them when interacting with you. Can you be blamed or held responsible for another's choice? You are only responsible for yours. If others choose not to come from a place of love inside themselves when in relationship with you, the error lies within them. They made the decision to come from a place of fear instead.

Only two states exist: love (spirit) or fear (ego). One is false and one is real. It is up to every individual to choose from which state they will come. It is not your job to make others come from a place of love. It is, however, your responsibility not to hinder in any way the process of another being able to exude love while in your presence. If being in your presence is not conducive to another having an experience of love, they must make a decision to honor their spirit. This is done by finding a person whose energy matches the vibration of their spirit. You must do the same.

If another chooses not to come from a place of love, it is because they do not know who they truly are. They do not know that they are spirit; they believe that they are ego. There is nothing you can do with those who are under this false illusion—they must awaken to the truth in their own time. If you choose to stay in a relationship with others who consistently come from a place of fear, you will eventually become tired of the resistance they mount to your experience of love. This will cause you to eventually end the relationship. Others are needed to have a relative experience of love. However, you may also choose to have an absolute experience of love, by choosing to access the love found within you directly, and giving it to yourself.

The truth has been realized—now accept it. Even after knowing the truth, many of you will choose not to accept it, as acceptance means giving up your false illusions. This you do not want to do, because who are you without your illusions? The question is, who are you *with* them? Your illusions have served your ego for so long that you loathe giving them up. You find the truth so unappealing. Who wants to give love to themselves? Where is the drama in that? There is little drama—no wonder it does not appeal to your ego.

But the time has come to either accept the whole truth or knowingly continue to serve your false ego. Who are you: spirit or ego? If you are spirit, then you are not without love. You can have an experience of love anytime you desire. Stop the madness you have created in the area of romantic relationships; replace that madness with sanity. Accept the truth and live it. You are made up of the very thing you seek the most. You are love; thus you can never be without it. Give up one of the greatest illusions on Earth: that love is acquired from another. Accept that it is not about what another gives to you, but what you give to yourself that matters.

Can you now understand why most romantic relationships on Earth fail? You erroneously believe that love is about what another gives to you, instead of what you give to yourself, and what others give to themselves. You diligently seek outside of yourself for love, because you perceive its imaginary absence. Your job is to supply love for yourself by understanding that you are a source of it. God, however, is the ultimate source of love.

Stop expressing love in your relationships with the unconscious motive of receiving it from another instead of from yourself. Use others as reference points in relationships when you desire a relative experience of love. Accept that others will use you as a reference point when they desire the same thing. This should clear up much of the confusion found in relationships. Men generally have always understood that in their experiences of love, their primary job was to give love to themselves; women need to realize this liberating truth as well. It is not selfish to give love to yourself when in a relationship with another. It is the only way love can be given: by you and to you.

Give up your ego-based relationships: they are based on the illusionary premise that another needs to fill perceived places of lack inside of you. Another can never fill a place lacking love inside of you, because you never lack love. You are merely unaware of the presence of love within you, when you are not tuned into your spirit. Love, understood in this context, is not a difficult or challenging thing—in fact it is quite the opposite. Love becomes easy to access, receive, and experience. Love was never meant to be something that you struggled to obtain; it is spirit operating from its own intrinsic nature.

All relationships are not of the romantic sort, although these relationships are the ones that trouble human beings the most. The most important relationship is the one you have with yourself. If you do not first take the time to tune into your spirit, the source of love found within you, then you will go without. You will go without love, that is. Human beings feel so devoid of love and hunger for love externally. But we do not take the time to receive it internally. Why is this? Can it be that you do not know how to fill yourself with the love found inside of you? How do you express love to others? Are you not kind, helpful, giving, comforting, and generous with them? Then express these same characteristics of spirit with yourself. Be kind, helpful, giving, comforting, generous, and accepting with and to yourself.

We are our worst critics—no one can condemn us worse than the voice inside our heads. This voice is false; it is constantly stating to us all of our perceived flaws and limitations. This voice is not a voice of love. You must withdraw your attention from it by connecting immediately with the presence of your spirit when this false voice speaks.

Spirit does not often speak; it serves as a quiet, reassuring presence in the background. Have you ever had times when you were in the midst of turmoil and felt peace anyway? This is your spirit attempting to surround you with the energy of love. When tumultuous times occur, we seek an answer to the question of why these challenging circumstances are happening. We reject the comfort of spirit at these times because its vibration does not match the energy of our conflicted nature. Instead, the peace that emanates from spirit tends to make us feel strange—it directly conflicts with our ego's perception of things. Is it not funny that we find peace an oddity, and yet conflict is considered to be the norm? Your spirit surrounds you silently, offering you its presence as a comfort in times of turmoil.

The only solution to any dilemma is love. You must take the time to consciously contact your spirit each and every day, and to remain aware of it throughout the day. Breath is a conduit to spirit, connecting you quickly to it. Breathing in deeply enables you to feel the presence of something else that is there. It makes you aware that you are surrounded by an energy field of love in which you reside. The desire for love is not unnatural—it is simply spirit's way of trying to draw your attention inward. Only there will you find the love you seek.

What are your fears about claiming your greatness?

19

Learning How to Relate to You

ONE IS DEEMED A LONELY number. A relationship, according to societal conditioning, is based on the notion of two. Cultivating a relationship with yourself seems unappealing and humdrum. Thus, we constantly seek to join with another, though at times we are better off being with just ourselves. The desire to be constantly in the presence of another is the ego attempting to provide itself with validation that it exists. Without receiving validation from another human being that we exist, we often feel invisible. The ego's claim of legitimacy erodes if there is no external witness to it. The one thing the ego fears is a still mind, devoid of thoughts. In mental stillness we come into contact with our spirit. This leads to us developing a meaningful relationship with ourselves.

Being with your spirit in mental silence is the first step in acquiring an authentic relationship with yourself. Initially, you will feel uncomfortable when you are mentally silent. Do nothing to remove yourself from the state of stillness you will find yourself in. Do not resist stillness—embrace it. After you get over these initial feelings, you will become more comfortable in the presence of silence. Your uncomfortable feelings arise from a fear of going into the unknown; the unknown entity you are coming into contact with is you.

You are an unknown entity to yourself. Are you interested in discovering who you truly are? This cannot be done unless you undertake the journey of your soul in the area of a relationship with self. This journey is an individual one—only you can take it. Why do you fear getting to know your authentic self? I believe it's because you are making a conscious choice to look inside yourself for the very first time. You are frightened because of your beliefs about yourself. Our fear is that nothing of value lies within us—surely we cannot receive the love we seek in some place as mundane as inside. How much fun is it to go within? Is it not more exciting to continue engaging in external dramas with the outer characters in our life?

The dramas created by the ego entertain us to a certain extent—if not, we would stop participating in them. It does not matter whether the dramas are happy ones; we enjoy the sad ones just as much, if not more. The sad ones confirm the truth about us: we are unworthy of the love we seek. Are we not? If not, why then do we insist on continuing a futile journey outside of ourselves? We are sure we know where love is to be found. Answer this question honestly: have you ever truly found love outside of yourself? If you responded "yes," the next question is: for how long? How much did it cost you? In the end, did you find it to be authentic? The love you find inside of yourself will complete you and allow you to feel whole. This love is authentic. Will you continue to linger on the precipice, or will you take a plunge into the unknown?

Decide to take a journey into the unknown depths of your soul. Many people delay making this journey. It is because of their refusal to give up hope that the self-created illusion of love being found with another is real. Until you are ready to give up this illusion you are attached to, you will delay the journey inside indefinitely. Only your spirit can liberate you from the illusions of the ego.

Before you begin the journey inside, you must have already done the work of forgiving all the characters in your dramas—including yourself—for not giving you what you felt you needed. Do not remain resentful, blaming others for what you feel they withheld from you. This keeps you attached to the hope that one day they will still give you what you feel you still need.

Forgiveness is the key to liberation. You must realize it was never the job of others to fill your emptiness with their love. You projected this onto others, and then condemned them when they did not act according to your wishes. The place that another decides to come from when they are with you depends on their level of conscious awareness about who they really are. A lack of forgiveness is merely a delaying mechanism, with the hidden purpose of preventing one from doing the inner work that needs to be done. Forgive yourself—and then others—for missing the mark, so you can start doing the internal work to authentically bring about your desires of the heart.

How does one forgive others? By knowing that they did not come to Earth to serve the purposes you assigned them. They came to pursue their own spiritual development; the manner and time in which they do so is completely up to them. Other people's spiritual development may not happen according to our timing. But this does not make them wrong—their obligation is to themselves first. If they choose to identify with themselves as ego instead of spirit, they are so entitled. You can no longer continue to blame people for being where they are in consciousness. They are where they have chosen to be, whether consciously or unconsciously. Forgive them.

As Christ said, "Father, forgive them; they don't know what they're doing."[1] Everyone has the God-given right to create one's own reality. At times our reality may differ from another's version of it. There is no one to blame when this occurs. Each person on Earth lives in his or her own world; sometimes worlds collide.

You forgive others when you accept the truth that they are entitled to live from their own truth and not yours. The next person you must forgive is yourself. You must forgive yourself for the attacks you levied towards others, both in your thoughts and in words. This you did because of the emotional wounds you erroneously blamed them for causing. You did not know at the time that you do not have the right to blame another for not giving you love in the manner you wanted. Either they were not aware of the source of love within them, or they did not choose you to reference in their experiences of acting from a place of love.

To continue blaming another for their choices means you believe they have something to give you—something you still need. Believing others withheld what you needed most is the cause of your pain. The pain you experience stems from the belief that love is lost to you. Love can never be lost, so blame others no more. Forgive yourself for the attacks you made on others based on illusions you once held about love. Know that another's job is not to support your illusions; it is *your* job to discover the truth about who you really are. Blame others no more, and blame yourself no more. You were not aware of the truth.

We live in a society where the truth is never taught about love: what it is and how to authentically experience it. You are as innocent as those whom you blamed for withholding it from you. You must allow people the freedom to show up in your life any way they wish to, without any expectations. Because in truth, no matter how much you try and get them to fit your image of how they should act in the drama called life, they never will. People are in your life for their own reasons and with their own agendas, as you are in theirs. Accept their choices, knowing you do not need them to be anything other than what they choose to be. The illusion of needing love from others has now been vanquished, sent back to the land of the ego from which it arose.

How can you continue to be in a relationship with those who, when they failed to live up to your expectations, received your blame? After you forgive them and yourself, give them the gift of freedom. Give them the freedom to show up in your life and act from whatever place they are in consciousness, without attacking them for being there. When others act in a manner not to your liking, do not be dismayed. You must do the work in your own consciousness to eradicate the need for a particular outcome or behavior. Ask yourself what illusions you are still holding on to, refusing to let die. Herein lies the problem—not what another is doing or not doing. The problem is your illusions and your attachment to them.

You must work diligently to give to yourself what you feel is missing in your life. The truth you do not wish to face is that it is up to you to do so. You tried to pass on to another the responsibility for your happiness, peace, and joy. You attempted to burden them with your needs and desires. Now you must assume the responsibility for filling the needy places within you. Return to a state of spirit inside yourself. This is the only place where your needs can be met: inside of you. Abdicating to another the responsibility for making us happy is what we have done up until now; we have now learned that this will result in sure failure. It is time for us to usher in a new dawn. We enter into the Promised Land when we realize that we alone have the power to fulfill our desires, and that no one else holds the key to our happiness.

The Promised Land is what its name suggests: a land promised to us by God where all of the desires of our heart will be fulfilled. What is the definition of land? We know it as property, earth, soil, and the ground. These are literal definitions. Metaphorically, land is an area in our consciousness—mental substance. Our consciousness is affected by the substance in which it finds itself, so who is in charge of this land (spirit or ego) is of vital importance. The Promised Land is the promise God makes to you that you will find a place of peace, rest, prosperity, and joy within. However, you still have to do the remaining work of ascending through 31 sublevels of consciousness in the Promised Land.

"Even when the way goes through Death Valley, I'm not afraid when you walk at my side."[2] The journey of the soul will cause you to walk through many valleys where the shadows of the dead lie. You will walk through dead states of being and thoughts in consciousness that used to represent who you were. Now all they do is cast a shadow. A shadow is cast when an image still remains, but only faintly. As you develop in consciousness, valleys of old, dead, ego thought systems may linger in your mind before they are completely eliminated from consciousness. Do not fear these shadows; all that is required is that you operate from a place of love.

Can shadows hurt you? They are not real—they are merely faint outlines of what used to be. Place no value on what used to be and is no more. When you are in lower levels of lands in your consciousness and shadows seek to scare you, walk confidently, knowing they have no power over you. Shadows are only remnants of darkness that appear to be frightening when there is little light. But when the light of your soul shines brightly, it will eliminate the shadows that once scared you. You will walk through many valleys of the shadow of death on the journey of your soul to the Promised Land. You will get stuck in the valleys of your life if you come from a place of fear when you are in them. Fear not; the I Am is with you. You will never be alone.

The valleys in your life represent times when you are in some type of emotional pain. There may be many reasons why you are experiencing pain. Pain is an indication that something has gone wrong. The individual circumstances causing you to feel pain are not important. What *is* important is that you are coming from a state contrary to the true and natural state of love found within you. Love, joy, and peace are natural states. If you are not in these states, something is wrong. You may occasionally experience short periods of pain and disharmony when faced with experiences you deem painful. But if you remain in pain over a long period of time, you are in a valley.

There is only one way to liberate yourself from the valley of pain you are in. You must find out which part of you is experiencing pain. Is your ego in pain, or is it your soul? Your spirit exists at a level higher than emotional pain. Your soul can experience pain if it is not continually coming from an awareness of love as the only reality. When your ego is in pain and, as a result, triggers your emotional pain body, to liberate yourself from this pain you must realize that you are not your ego. The ego being in pain has nothing to do with the real you. You can observe the pain it is feeling—but at the same time you recognize that another part of you, your spirit, is somewhere else, not in pain. Choose to align yourself with your spirit when your ego is in pain. Make a conscious decision to identify only with your spirit when being emotionally bombarded with stimuli that your ego finds painful.

When your soul identifies with the ego, and thus is in pain, it will experience feelings of frustration and being stuck in some way. When the state of love emanating from your spirit is being restrained in some way. That is the cause of the unease you are feeling in your soul.

The only way to free yourself is to remove what is blocking the flow of love in you. It may be a person, a particular situation, a job, or something you fear facing. Regardless of what it is, you are being blocked from emanating from a place of love within you; the blockage must be removed. The highest purpose of your soul is to express itself as love on

Earth. It bears repeating that whatever is preventing you from doing this must be eliminated.

You may have to remove your own self if you are blocking your spirit from expressing love. The self that you must eliminate is the ego. You are not fear, pain, hurt, anger, blame, a victim, or a victimizer—you are none of these things. Identifying with and coming from a place of ego may cause you to act from these false states of being. You in fact are love, peace, joy, forgiveness, and gratitude. Moving external and internal blocks that prevent love from flowing freely within you, to outside of you and into the world, is the work that needs to be done.

It is understandable that at times you find it difficult to come from a place of love, because you are experiencing challenging conditions. However, you must make it your duty to return to a state of love as quickly as possible. Signs that you have lingered outside of love for too long occur when you experience feelings of apathy, numbness, hurt, anger, resentment, sadness, hopelessness, cold-heartedness, and unhappiness. When you are experiencing these emotions over an extended period of time, you are out of the energy of love.

You must do whatever work is takes to return to a state of love within yourself. Remove whatever blocks you from doing so. Love must flow from within to without. When you release the energy of love into the universe, more love flows back to you. When you become disconnected from the source of love inside you, thus identifying with yourself as an ego, you are in the valley of the shadow of death.

Do not despair: God is with you, and will serve as the light you follow to lead you out of the valleys in your life. Focus your attention on God and surrender your feelings of pain; he will lead you home, back to a place of love. It does not matter if you have previously alienated yourself from God and deny his presence of love within you, or that you lay the blame at his doorstep for being in a valley in the first place. He will still aid you. God is with you, and his presence that you connect with inside will provide you with comfort.

We must learn to allow the I Am to comfort us while we are in pain. God longs to do so. To keep your pain to yourself is a selfish decision; it denies God the opportunity to heal you. Sometimes pain is the only thing that makes you feel alive. But the only true stimulus you need to feel alive is love. Delay no further: invite the I Am in and ask God to heal you of the pain you are experiencing. He will do so. Cling to the cloak of protection that he offers you.

It may take a little while before you can accept the solace God offers. This delay stems from the fact that you have been too long out of the energy of love. Your concerted efforts to reach God will eventually allow you to connect to his presence within you. Surrendering undesirable states of being is something that must take place on a daily basis; you must die regularly to false states.

After you surrender emotional or physical pain, allow God to heal you. There is no better balm for your wounds than the presence of God. The presence of God and his love is the salve being applied to your wounds. God will apply it generously, and you will heal. Allow this process to occur. How long it takes is irrelevant; what *is* important is that at the end of this time of healing, you will be returned to a state of love inside of yourself.

After the pain is gone, you will not immediately feel the love inside you. You will still feel a bit numb after the pain has been healed. If you allow yourself to connect regularly with spirit at this time, the embers of love will begin to flicker in you once again. You allow the embers of love to ignite brightly within you through nurturing them by performing loving acts. The flame of love inside you can never truly go out, but the light of your spirit within can be dimmed when you are in the valleys of your life. When you can once again come from a place of love inside of yourself, you are ready to leave the valley.

Do not fear valleys, for they serve a useful purpose. They afford you the opportunity to remove the blockage that is keeping you from experiencing yourself as spirit. You will have valley experiences even in the Promised Land; how long you remain in them is up to you. The key to facilitating the transition back to a place of love is extending forgiveness to yourself and all others.

COMPASS

What will it take for you to authentically love yourself?

20

Where Are You?

IF YOU ARE NOT OFTEN in a joyful state, something is blocking its expression in you. You must remove the blockage in your consciousness as quickly as possible. Joy is your birthright—it is spirit expressing its state of being. When one is experiencing joy, they often act childlike. Often, when you show what others deem to be too much joy and excitement, it makes them feel uncomfortable. Others seek to temper your joy—do not let them. It is because they are disconnected from their spirit. The apparent connection you have to your own spirit makes others feel their own lack of connection more keenly, so they express irritation when you act joyful. Most people are unconscious of the real cause of the irritation they feel.

Where Are You?

So many people on Earth seem to be living without joy. Material wealth does not bring about joy, and neither does the outer fulfillment of our desires. Misunderstanding the origins of joy prevents it from being felt authentically. If people knew that joy is a natural state of being stemming from a source of love inside of them when they are connected to their spirit, then they would feel it all the time, regardless of outer conditions in their lives. If joy is accessible to all, why do more people not utilize this gift? Why are so many people choosing to live a life devoid of joy? People have become so comfortable living in a joyless state—joy is seen as unnatural, whereas sadness is seen as acceptable. You do that which you become used to doing. Expressing joy has to become habitual. When it becomes routine to come from joy, it will become natural to you.

Why is joy important? When you do not live in a state of joy, you will attract outer experiences that mirror your inner state of joylessness. You attract into your life a host of circumstances, events, people, and situations that are equivalent to your inner state of being. Joy attracts joy, while its antithesis—sadness—attracts into your life conditions you will find sorrowful. The energy of your inner state acts like a magnet, drawing to you experiences that match the level of its vibration. You determine the circumstances of your life based on the choices you make, whether conscious or not. If you choose joy, joy will choose you. Joy is a precious gift; allow it to flow freely from the wellspring of spirit bubbling in you. In the Promised Land you must be ready to make the choice to allow joy in.

We have talked about the stages of spiritual development or plateaus one reaches in their consciousness. Let us discuss the different life areas where these developments take place. One such area is in your professional life. Another is in the area of personal relationships and the relationship with self. Your home life is another area where development occurs; acquiring a prosperity consciousness is yet another.

Knowing where you are in consciousness in every aspect of your life is important for a number of reasons. Becoming aware of what you need to work on spiritually to evolve will make it easier to evolve in consciousness. For example, if in your personal life you need to work on acquiring more self-love, knowing this may help you understand why you may be in an emotionally or physically abusive relationship. Realizing what your soul seeks to experience on Earth in order to develop will make the spiritual work you came to do much easier.

You can be concurrently at different levels of spiritual development in each area of your life. For example, you can be in Egypt in your personal life, yet in your professional life you are in the Promised Land. You can simultaneously have two different experiences of conscious development in disparate life areas. The lessons you learn in areas where you are more spiritually developed may assist you in areas where you are not as highly developed. Knowing where you are in consciousness is the first step; determining what is needed to acquire a higher state of consciousness in each area of your life is the next step.

Here are some general guidelines to help you acquire a higher level of consciousness in all areas of your life. Always be truthful to yourself about where you are in consciousness at every moment. Make no apologies to yourself—or anyone else—about where you are in consciousness. As my former minister was fond of saying, the key is "self-observation without condemnation." Accepting where you are now is the fastest way to get where you are going. You are where you are for a reason: there is something here that you must learn. Focusing on learning the lessons sent to you, as opposed to being caught up in the drama of the experience, is how you evolve more quickly.

It is important to understand that there is no external penalty imposed if you choose to remain where you are in consciousness without evolving any further. If you refuse to do the work necessary for evolution, the only consequence is remaining in your present state of consciousness.

Where Are You?

This might seem acceptable—but imagine staying where you are in consciousness for the rest of your life, with no potential for growth. Divine assistance is always ready to help you and guide your spiritual evolution. You must be open to change, willing to allow old states of being that no longer represent your current self to fade away.

Know that you are doing the best you can at every minute (unless you are choosing not to). Only you can determine this. Beating up on yourself and feeling guilty about your progress will only serve to defeat you. Having compassion for yourself on the journey of the soul is a must. Monitoring your spiritual progression in each life area is beneficial. Studying spiritual literature is useful in developing your consciousness. Don't avoid situations which scare you—developing a spirit of courage will greatly help you to evolve spiritually.

What does it look like, being in different places in consciousness in various areas of your life? It looks like your life right now. Have you taken the time recently to examine it? If you do so, you will observe that you are more successful in one life area than another. Some people may find their lives to be equally evolved in every area, but this is rare. Most people have chosen to give more attention to one life area than another, so they will have achieved a greater measure of success in this area. Typically it is in the life area of work.

Make a list of all the areas in your life. Determine where you are spiritually in each one. Are you in Egypt, the Red Sea, the Wilderness, the Jordan River, or the Promised Land stages of spiritual development? Or have you reached the level of Christ Consciousness? After you determine what stage of development you are in, ask yourself what you need to work on to evolve further. You can determine this by making a list of what you have learned thus far in each area of your life, and what lessons still elude you. You will be surprised to learn how much you already know about yourself if you are honest throughout this process.

Taking inventory of your consciousness on a regular basis will help you raise your awareness more rapidly. As Socrates once said, "The unexamined life is not worth living." Examine each area of your life, and do the work necessary to ascend higher in spiritual awareness in each life area. The result will be a rewarding and fulfilling experience of life. But the ultimate reward is learning to accept your divinity: there can be no greater reward than coming to know yourself as God.

Why embark at all on the journey of the soul? This is a question that many of us who have been on the spiritual path for many years have started to ask ourselves. Many of us might not feel more of anything for having undertaken the journey. Our pot of gold overflowing with happiness, love, peace, joy, and prosperity still eludes us. We often wonder why we have spent so much time and worked so hard to develop spiritually—only to be slightly better off than before we began the journey. Our journey is not yet over; what you seek, you will find. However, you might not find it in the way, manner, or the time frame you wish.

God's promise to you is that you will receive the desires of your heart. The problem is that human beings evolve in consciousness incredibly slowly—it seems that we evolve an inch at a time. It may look to you like little spiritual progress has been made because it has taken a long time for you to arrive where you are in consciousness. What is important is that you have evolved *somewhat* in your consciousness. The time it took for you to evolve is not as important as the fact that evolution has taken place.

You can get weary of the journey: it calls for you to surrender so much. You have been called to surrender your dreams, your hopes, and all of your Earthly desires. What have you received in return? You can call yourself somewhat more spiritually evolved, but at this stage in the journey this may feel like an empty reward. Does being more spiritually evolved allow you to experience love, joy, and peace for a sustained period of time? To many at this point of the journey, the answer is still no. What, then, is the reward for undertaking the journey of the soul? Have you come to believe that there is none, other than the lessons learned on the way? God will answer your silent plea for understanding.

The journey was undertaken with another silent plea with which you beseeched God: "Please help me to learn the truth. Please help me to end all of the suffering and needless pain I feel." Help me, God, to be at a higher state of conscious understanding, is what you were really asking for. At the time, though, you did not know this; you understand it only now.

In order to answer your plea, the I Am first had to remove you from where you were in consciousness. But you stubbornly refused to be moved—you clung to old and familiar ways of being, though they were the very things holding you trapped in a vicious cycle of emotional pain. Your thoughts are the nails that hold you confined to the heavy crosses in your life that you bear upon the back of your spirit. The only way for the nails to be removed is to allow your ego to be crucified and resurrected anew as spirit. Then, out from your ashes, your spirit will rise in conscious flight and assume a place of dominance in your thoughts.

The problem is that the ego refuses to remain crucified; it somehow finds a way to resurrect itself. You permit it to do so because it still offers a promise of some illusory reward that you still hunger for. Spirit will not intercede on your behalf in your dealings with your ego. It is only after once again becoming enslaved to the ego that you discover the truth. The ego and all of its promises are not real. All that the ego promises to deliver either fails to materialize or—if it materializes—leaves you unfulfilled. So once again, you seek out God with a silent plea for help, and you resume the journey of the soul.

What have you learned since the beginning of your journey? You may not have acquired your heart's desires yet, but you learned something quite valuable: that you are a source of love. This may not seem terribly important in proportion to all of the suffering and hard work you had to endure on the journey. But, my friend, it is. To know that you are an authentic source of love for yourself, and that love can be found within you, means you can no longer be without love again.

To know this truth is liberating. Now you can free yourself from the biggest weapon in the ego's arsenal: a hunger for external love and recognition. You are now released from the prison that once held you captive. You have attained the key to your salvation. You have love. You need beg no more for it—love is found inside of you. That alone is worth the price you paid to get to where you are on the journey.

I see you still do not believe me. How could this seemingly small gift be worth all you have endured? I will tell you how. First you must understand that you are not the same person as when you first undertook the journey of the soul; you have been irrevocably changed. You have evolved into a higher state of being, where you now know yourself to be spirit. The vacillating back and forth between the ego and spirit has ended. You question your identity no more. You know in quiet certainty, "I am spirit. This is my only identity."

Being in this state of awareness allows you to enter a place where you come into contact with the energy of love, thus allowing you to experience your authentic spiritual self even more fully. You become a witness to the love that emanates from you when you share it with others. This offers you an opportunity to have a relative experience of yourself as spirit. You realize that spirit is capable of acting in a loving manner even when faced with people and situations that challenge your peace. You call to yourself many of these situations in order to give yourself the opportunity to express the truth of your divinity. This strengthens your spiritual muscles, so to speak.

Let us reiterate the rewards of taking the journey. Without love of self you can never acquire the desires of your heart. You come to love yourself when you start to identify with yourself as spirit. This is the gift you unknowingly sought to give yourself with your plea to God. What you were praying to the I Am for was to help you love yourself, and to get to know the real you better. For the I Am knew that once you did this, you would never thirst outside of yourself for love again. The I Am beckoned you from within to embark on the journey of the soul.

Can you still tell me that the price you paid was not worth it? Self-love is an immeasurable gift. It is the cornerstone of your conscious development; without it you would never be ready to join in union with your spirit. I know that self-love may not seem particularly rewarding in and of itself, but it is the highest reward God can offer you.

God gave you the most valuable gift that he could. Are you now ready to accept it? The gift of self-love is the same gift the Creator gave to himself. By becoming aware of the love he is made of, and by immersing himself in the energy of that love, the Creator became one with it. By placing love into action, the Creator created a field of energy where love could be experienced. The awareness of oneself as love creates an ever-expanding field of eternal love. In this way was the Universe, and everything in it, made.

This is how you too can create the universe in which you live. One can create the physical world in which they live based on their connection to the source of love found within. Do you not see that the only gift God could give to you is the same one God gave to himself: the gift of love? Do you realize the enormity of this gift? By authentically acquiring self-love, you can consciously have the experience of yourself as God. This is the reward you have so justly earned by agreeing to undertake the journey of your soul. Your reward is the growing awareness of your divinity. Enjoy and rise in conscious awareness of this gift.

There are other rewards for undertaking the journey and working so diligently to develop your consciousness, but the primary gift is that of self-love. To love and to know yourself as spirit is to have the world quite literally at your feet. When you are clear about who you are, others and outer circumstances will no longer adversely affect you. We are only affected by outer circumstances when there is still a lingering question about who we are. Your response to the question, "who am I?" should now be consistently the same: "I am love. I am spirit. I am God."

You may persist in the belief that self-love is not an important gift. This is because a part of you is still attached to the ego's obsession with acquiring love from someone other than yourself. Do not allow the ego's false illusions to reside in you anymore. Claim your reward and declare in victory, "I am spirit. I am love. I am God." Then, after declaring this, demonstrate it as truth. That is the reason why you came to Earth: to give yourself an experience of being God. You were never meant to give yourself an experience of being an ego. The ego is a false god created in ignorance and anonymity by the mind. The ego emerges when you seek to understand the nature of your existence purely from a materialistic viewpoint. Because the ego was created by the mind, there is where it must be buried. Take your mind back—free it from the grips of insanity. It is insane to allow the ego to continue running amok.

The reward the journey offers after you come to know yourself as love is to evolve even further, and to begin to know yourself as the Christ. The Christ Consciousness stage of spiritual development is a stage where you are in complete oneness and union with God. In this stage you come to know that you too are God. You get to this stage by demonstrating higher expressions of yourself as love, through a multitude of experiences.

At the Christ Consciousness stage of development you no longer need outer experiences in order to demonstrate to yourself who you are. This is the stage where you know without question that you are divine, and you are connected to the highest state of love which is found within you. Jesus came as a soul to Earth in order to provide you a template to use in acquiring the consciousness of the Christ. This template is available for your use; fill in the blanks with your own individual life circumstances.

Those who have not chosen Christ as their guide can use other templates left by other master wayshowers; Buddha left such a template. How you fill in the blanks is up to you. Know, however, that as you seek to evolve, you can use the template left by master wayshowers, or you can create your own original template. Jesus did not come to Earth fully evolved; he came at the very end stages of spiritual development, to share with us the means by which we too could obtain Christ Consciousness. We are divine spirit using Earth as a learning facility to give ourselves relative experiences, which in turn increase our understanding of love as our true identity.

COMPASS

What is your connection to God, the Creator, or a Higher Power like?

21

Every Master Takes the Journey

ALL SOULS TAKE A JOURNEY—that is what they do by their very nature. How many of us even recognize that we have a soul, and that it takes a journey? This journey is one taken into the depths of our individual consciousness. Each successive stage of spiritual development we reach on our journey moves us higher in consciousness, further along on our spiritual path. The experiences we encounter on the way will help us grow.

The ultimate purpose of the journey of the soul is to awaken to our true identity as spirit. Because spirit is made up of millions of intricate facets, we come to know ourselves through experiencing each facet, individually as a soul. We are able to have multiple soul experiences at the same time.

There are six stages of spiritual development: Egypt, the Red Sea, the Wilderness, the Jordan River, and the Promised Land. When all of these stages have been attained in consciousness, you then develop the Christ level of consciousness. This is the last stage of spiritual development before unification with God. This level is not so much another stage of development as it is the sum total, the end product of all the other stages.

Why is learning about these stages important? If you know where you are in consciousness, you can better serve your own spiritual progression.

The first step in spiritual development is awareness. You must be aware of where you are on your journey by monitoring where you are in consciousness in every area of your life. The right location—as in real estate—is the key to success. The property we are referring to is your consciousness. Where you are, and what stage of conscious development you are in, is the key to successfully evolving spiritually. The investment you make in yourself will pay huge dividends if your consciousness is in a prime location. Is your consciousness in Egypt, the Red Sea, the Wilderness, the Jordan River, the Promised Land, or have you reached Christ Consciousness?

Let us briefly revisit each stage of spiritual development we will encounter on our journey. You are in Egypt when you are still preoccupied with the material and the means for basic survival: a job, a house, money, a basic education, and so forth. You cross the Red Sea when you choose, through an act of faith, to leave Egypt and head into unfamiliar territory. You answer the call of your soul to take a journey. It urges you to leave what has become familiar to you, and seek spiritual fulfillment. By taking a great leap of faith into the unknown, you embark on a miraculous journey of your soul.

You then enter the Wilderness stage of development. In the Wilderness phase you begin a conscious relationship with your Creator.

You lose identification with yourself as a material being, since your identity is stripped away due to a lack of focused attention on the material. After your identity—established in society by your level of material success—is gone, you will come to realize that you still exist. You make first contact with yourself as a spiritual being. You wander in the Wilderness for a lengthy period of time, depending on how long it takes for a new generation of spiritual thoughts to emerge in your consciousness. In the Wilderness, you will be shown your spiritual purpose in life.

After you learn your spiritual purpose, you enter into the Jordan River stage. In the Jordan you work hard in the outer world—as hard as you worked on your inner development in the Wilderness. In the Jordan River you will be asked to step out on faith based on the directive given to you by God. You must put your faith to the test. It is not enough to simply have faith in God; you must demonstrate it routinely through your outer actions. You will experience frequent miracles in the Jordan River.

After you have seen the Jordan River stage through to completion, you reach the Promised Land. Here in the Promised Land stage of spiritual development, what has been promised to you by God manifests in your physical reality, though it does not necessarily manifest in the manner or time you would prefer. The rewards of spirit will now yield fruit because you have brought forward the inner conditions necessary for manifestation to occur outwardly. What you will be able to outwardly manifest will increase in proportion to the level of your spiritual development. The Promised Land is not a land of "wide-open spaces, a land lush with milk and honey"[1] as you may think—at least not in its beginning levels.

There are 31 sublevels, or lower thought systems, that you have to overcome in your consciousness. These lower thought systems are the rulers or kings in your mind that claim ownership over different aspects that make up your consciousness. They must be overthrown. You can only overthrow each king in consciousness by challenging the stronghold it has established in your mind. You must reclaim your mind for its intended purpose as a tool of the spirit. The promised milk and honey will be partaken of only after you conquer the interlopers in your mind. After you evolve through each of the successive 31 lower-level thought systems in your mind, you will reach the Christ Consciousness stage.

Each time you overthrow a king you gain new territory, thus clearing a wide-open space in your consciousness. But you must leave this territory after it becomes familiar and comfortable; you must start the journey of the soul over again in the same area of your life. For example, you cannot conquer Ai, a new land, simply because you were successful in conquering Jericho. Your consciousness, though victorious in overthrowing Jericho, cannot acquire Ai. You must go back and acquire a higher degree of consciousness in a particular life area before you will be ready to conquer Ai.

After you have conquered a new land, it becomes Egypt to you again. This occurs when you have claimed all its territory as your own and you have nothing more to gain. After claiming victory, it is time to move on. You have many more lands and territories to conquer in your consciousness. When your spirit starts to nudge you to move again, you know that your sojourn in the land you have conquered is now over. It is time to continue the journey of the soul. You do this by leaving Egypt and going through the stages of spiritual development again, until you reach the subsequent sublevel in the Promised Land.

The journey of the soul is cyclical in nature. With each new cycle you undertake, you retain the knowledge you gained previously, thus making it somewhat easier for you to venture back into familiar lands in consciousness. Although the lands will seem familiar, your way of perceiving them will not be. You will be looking at these lands through the eyes of one who is learning to become a master of consciousness.

Every Master Takes the Journey

The illusion you must give up when called to move to higher ground in consciousness is the notion that all of your spiritual work is already done. Your work is never done as long as you are still alive. As long as you are living, you will be called to experience higher and higher aspects of yourself.

If you refuse to leave where you are in consciousness, spirit will have no choice but to move you by force, i.e., challenging circumstances. Why not go willingly into new land? Do you remember your previous journey—what happened when you delayed before? Are you reluctant to move because you feel complacent, or is it because you are afraid to proclaim who you really are? There is nowhere left for you to hide. Your light will now become visible to all. There can be no more delaying tactics. The time will come to proclaim: "I too am God—part of the whole and yet an individual facet of the divine."

The archetype of each of these six stages of spiritual development is found in every major religion. Every major religious figure, regardless of the religion, has undergone the journey of the soul. You can use their experiences as a blueprint to help you on your own journey. The stages of spiritual development are universal and exemplified by any religious model. I personally have chosen to view through the lens of Christianity. A Buddhist, a Hindu, a Jew, a Muslim, a Mormon, or a student of any other religion can easily acquaint themselves with these stages of development through the similar journey that the central figures in their own religion took.

If the stages of spiritual development are looked at through a Buddhist model, the life of the Buddha can be understood through these six stages of spiritual development. Siddhartha lived in a world of tremendous material wealth, and the focus of his everyday life was on the material world. Siddhartha was being groomed for a leadership role in his kingdom; his roles in life were that of prince, husband, father, and dutiful son. His entire existence was from a materialistic reference point. He was in the Egypt stage of spiritual development.

A sense of restlessness and a feeling of there being more to life arose from within Siddhartha; his spirit was urging him to undertake the journey of the soul. This urging led Siddhartha to wander outside his palace walls. When he ventured outside, he encountered human suffering for the first time. This experience removed the veil of illusion Siddhartha had lived under; for the first time he was introduced to death. He decided to leave his world of materiality, venturing into the unknown to seek fulfillment and a higher way of existence. This "Great Going Forth," through a leap of faith, was Siddhartha's Red Sea experience.

Siddhartha wandered for many years seeking spiritual fulfillment. During his Wilderness experience he studied with famous Brahmins. He lost all identification with his human facade, and began to identify with himself as spirit. After developing a relationship with the divine and gaining spiritual knowledge, he was ready to leave the Wilderness and enter the Jordan River stage of spiritual development.

In the Jordan River, Siddhartha shared the spiritual knowledge he had acquired in the Wilderness with those who began to follow him. He became known as a great spiritual teacher, and entered the Promised Land. His spirit urged him to acquire even higher spiritual awareness. He left the Promised Land, which had become Egypt to him. He recommenced the journey of the soul, moving through the successive stages of spiritual development until he reached the Promised Land at the next successive sublevel of spiritual development.

Siddhartha in due course obtained enlightenment, and became the Buddha. This is said to have occurred when he sat under a Bodhi tree for a period of time. He developed his philosophy of "the Middle Way" and desired to share all that he had learned with others. By guiding others on the path to enlightenment he reached Buddhahood, or the Christ Consciousness stage of spiritual development.

Every Master Takes the Journey

Every religion offers a blueprint of the stages of spiritual development. The Book of Mormon chronicles the journey of the soul of the prophet Lehi and his family. Lehi and his family were led by God to leave their home and their material possessions, through a vision given to Lehi about imminent destruction of the land where he lived. Lehi left the Egypt stage of spiritual development when he heeded the call of spirit to leave home.

Lehi's leap of faith, following a vision given by God, was his Red Sea experience. He and his family wandered in the Wilderness. He received guidance from a divine compass of sorts (Liahona), given to him by God. The guidance was dependent on Lehi's (and his family's) steadfast faith and obedience to God. Lehi entered the Jordan River stage when, following the directive given to him by God—by faith alone—he had a boat built and crossed the ocean on it.

God led Lehi and his family to the Promised Land. Once there, some of his family—in particular his two eldest sons and their wives—had to split or part ways with his remaining family in order for spiritual advancement to take place. This symbolizes the aspects of our consciousness we must part with, even after we enter the Promised Land, in order to develop further. Those aspects of our consciousness unwilling to evolve into higher forms of awareness must be parted with.

In both the Jewish and Christian religions, the journey of the soul is demonstrated through the life of Moses. Moses was an Egyptian prince; he had great material wealth and power. He is said to have given up his world of materiality because of an act he committed that caused him to leave Egypt. Leaving Egypt and venturing into the unknown was his Red Sea experience. He was led and sustained by spirit in the Wilderness. In the Wilderness, Moses wandered until he was 80 years old, until he no longer identified with his ego or a materialistic form of existence. God gave Moses his spiritual mission in life: to lead the Hebrew people out of bondage in Egypt.

Moses entered the Jordan River phase of spiritual development when he reentered the outer world and began to perform miracles. Although apprehensive, he stepped out in faith by obediently heeding God's decree. An example of this is when he overcame his purported fear of speaking in public. God challenged Moses' limiting self-beliefs. Moses was shown what God is capable of doing through us—if we allow ourselves to be used.

Moses entered into the Promised Land of spiritual development within his own consciousness. He did not enter into the Promised Land in the physical sense, on Earth; he fulfilled his spiritual mission with God by preparing his people to enter the land promised to them by God. His Earthly work done, Moses reached the Christ Consciousness stage of spiritual development and ascended into the heavens.

There is also the journey of the soul that Jesus took before he became the Christ. Jesus was different in the sense that he came to Earth already aware of his identity as spirit. As a result, it was not necessary for him to go through the Egypt stage of spiritual development. There is a famous story about Jesus as a young boy. He decided to leave his parents' house and instead spent the day at Temple. His parents had been looking for him and were worried, so when they found him they questioned him about his whereabouts. His response was, "Why were you looking for me? Didn't you know that I had to be here, dealing with the things of my Father?"[2] He never had to cross the Red Sea of faith into conscious remembrance; he remembered early on who he really was. He did not identify with his Earthly parents as much as with his heavenly father.

Jesus originated his journey of the soul in the Wilderness phase. Not much is known about his whereabouts during this period—it is called his "lost years." Wherever he wandered in the Wilderness, we know his journey was of an inner nature. In the Wilderness, Jesus became fully awakened to his divinity and purpose in life; he also developed a strong and unifying relationship with God. The Bible mentions that he once spent 40 days and nights in the Wilderness, where he prayed and meditated. In the Wilderness we are called upon to give up our lower thoughts for higher ones, but we are tempted by the ego to remain attached to a lower way of thinking. This was exemplified in the Wilderness when Jesus' adversarial thoughts proved unsuccessful in thwarting him from his chosen path.

When Jesus decided to start his ministry on Earth, he was baptized in the River Jordan by John the Baptist; thus he began his work in the Jordan River stage of spiritual development. The first thing Jesus did was to call to him 12 disciples, or to awaken his 12 spiritual powers. Jesus and his disciples were called upon to do challenging work in the outer world. He performed noted miracles. He sought to teach others about the true nature of God, and to dissuade people from strict outer adherence to spiritual law. This work was often very dangerous; it threatened his physical life. Nonetheless, he held to his course set by God.

Jesus was often called to do seemingly impossible tasks, such as healing the sick and raising the dead. He demonstrated absolute truth over any illusion that stood in his way. However, Jesus did have a fully human experience while on Earth. Some of his struggles to overcome the lower levels of his mind can be seen in the garden of Gethsemane, and also on the cross when he asked, "My God, my God, why have you abandoned me?"[3] Ultimately, Jesus did not allow lower-energy fearful thinking to besiege him for too long. He quickly raised his consciousness and aligned himself with the higher will of God.

Jesus entered the Promised Land stage of spiritual development when he came to his own personal realization that he was the son of God. Others outwardly speculated on his identity, but it is important that Jesus came to this realization *himself*. When Jesus accepted this truth, he entered into the Promised Land. What was promised to him was a level of consciousness where he would fulfill his divine potential: a conscious awareness that he was the living Son of God.

Jesus' decision to be a willing participant in life (and ultimately physical death) enabled him to become the fully evolved Christ. He surrendered what was left of his human personality. He became the Christ, and he reached the Christ Consciousness stage of spiritual development. By transcending the illusory limitations that death places on life, he was able to demonstrate mastery over the greatest illusion of them all: physical death. Jesus' journey of the soul was over. It had led him to complete reunion with the I Am as the Christ. Jesus then became Jesus the Christ.

Each religion has its own examples of religious figures going through the six stages of development in their own personal journeys of the soul. You can chart the spiritual development of the prophet Muhammad in the Islamic religion. In Hinduism you can study the journey of any of its deities, such as Krishna and Rama. Whichever religion you believe in—whatever religious teacher, prophet, or child of God you choose to believe in—remember: what is important is that you use their lives as reference points to aid you in determining where you are on the journey of your soul.

Where you are spiritually in every area of your life is important. Chart your own course of spiritual progression: where are you now in your personal life, work life, and in relationships, including the one with yourself? By knowing where you are in consciousness, you will understand where you are going, where you have been, and why you are there. Knowledge is the key to understanding, understanding is the key to achieving, and achieving is the key to becoming. The journey of the soul will help bring about the realization of your true identity: as spirit.

COMPASS

Is there a blueprint for the journey of the soul that a teacher, deity, prophet, or leader in your religion took? How can you use their journey to aid you in yours?

22

The Illusions to Be Surrendered

AT EACH STAGE OF SPIRITUAL development you are asked to give up something that no longer serves you. Each stage is not merely about learning and developing in each life area; it also involves giving something up. In other words, you are asked to give up the illusions you have created in place of truth in every area of your life. When you are ready to accept these illusions as false, you will be ready to replace illusion with truth. You will be called to give up illusions in whatever stage of spiritual development you are working on in your life.

The first major illusion you must give up when you are in Egypt is in the area of work. The ego assigns you value through your body, status, bank account, job, education, and material possessions. When you are near the end of the Egypt phase, these things will no longer represent who you feel you are. In fact, you begin to feel more alienated from these things as having anything to do with who you truly are. So the first major illusion you give up is the one that says, "I am what I materially produce in the world." Giving up this illusion prepares you to begin your journey of the soul, and to give up lower-level thinking for higher-order thinking.

The illusion you give up in the Red Sea phase is one that life is just the way it is, and that there is nothing you can do to make it better. A sense of complacency about the conditions in your life through acceptance and passivity is what needs to be challenged. You must replace this illusion with the truth that sometimes, in order to make things better, you may first have to give it all up. In the Red Sea you will take a leap of faith into the unknown, challenging the belief that there is nothing you can do to make your life better. You realize that, in fact, you are not stuck. Being stuck was the illusion that your ego was feeding you. You choose to listen to your spirit calling you to move to higher ground in consciousness.

When you enter into the Wilderness phase, you begin to lose identification with yourself as a material being, since you lose your material possessions and titles. Because you can no longer define yourself as a material being, you discover the truth that you are really "a spiritual being having a human experience." Giving up this illusion allows you to relate to yourself as spirit.

In the Wilderness there is another great illusion you must give up: the belief that you are in control of your life. In the Wilderness, your attempts to control life events will fail. You will not be able to exercise control over the outer events in your life—at least, not to your liking. The ego fights hard to hold onto its illusion of controlling events, circumstances, and people according to its wishes. The work to be done in the Wilderness is to strip the ego of this erroneous belief; how long this will take depends on how strongly you remain attached to the need for outer control. The longer you delay in doing so, the more needless suffering you will go through.

You will stop looking to yourself as the source of anything; you will instead learn to depend on God as the only source. This does not mean you do not play an important role in sustaining yourself—it means that your role will become secondary to God's. Learning to depend on a higher power is the truth you must realize and accept in place of faith in your own ability to manifest whatever you desire. What served you so well in Egypt—your ability to control outer events—will now fail you in the Wilderness.

This will be hard for many to accept. You have much invested in the belief in your ego's ability to shape everything in your life just the way you like it. If holding onto this false power is still so important to you, you will remain in the Wilderness much longer than necessary. You may even choose to leave it at this point and return to Egypt. The Wilderness is a place for those who are ready to stop playing illusory games. The only real power is the power of spirit—everything else is a child at play in the world of make believe.

In the Wilderness you will come to the realization, "I can no longer do anything without God and his guidance." This is actually a liberating thing—in truth, if you are honest with yourself, the thought that everything was dependent on you was terrifying. It gave you feelings of being burdened with a load that was impossible to carry. Dependency on God has its rewards: the burdens of life are lifted from your shoulders and placed onto one easily capable of carrying them.

God does not demand dependency for his sake, but for yours. A dependent being is one who knows that everything in the world is built on the foundation of spirit. Dependency on God is a mere acknowledgement that the Creator of all supports you. God will not wrest surrender away from you. If you insist on holding onto your perceived illusion of having power and control, life circumstances will wrest your illusions from you. Do not view this as punishment, but as a compassionate Universe trying to get you to realize the truth: that God is in control of your life and affairs.

In the Jordan River stage, you will be called to give up your false belief in the power of the ego. You will have to act from a new sense of power; the source of this new power will be your indwelling spirit. You must challenge and give up another illusion that is plaguing you: the voice in your head that says you are not enough. You believe that you are not intelligent enough, worthy enough, deserving enough, perfect enough, or beautiful enough for your good to manifest.

The Jordan River phase is the place where you will successfully demonstrate the miraculous in the physical world; you will successfully overcome the notion of impossibility. You will discover a great power within yourself that you can access at will, which will make all things possible through faith.

When you reach the Promised Land stage, you must give up the illusion that you have arrived, that everything from this point on will now be easy. You will soon realize that this is not the truth—the Promised Land provides ample opportunities for your spiritual growth. It brings forth situations that challenge specific areas within you that are still in need of spiritual development. Although life does get somewhat easier in the Promised Land, it will never become easy—there will always be work for you to do.

The work of evolving never stops and is exponential in nature: the higher you evolve, the more advanced your consciousness. Think of your consciousness as a sphere continuously revolving around itself, creating ever-increasing, larger spheres of knowledge. Within each sphere you experience higher and higher levels of spiritual awareness, causing you to expand into even greater dimensions of yourself.

What illusions do you need to give up that you are still holding onto?

23

The Greatest Illusion

ILLUSIONS NO LONGER SERVE A purpose in your life, since you have ceased to identify with yourself as ego. When you reach the Christ Consciousness stage of spiritual development, you will have given up all of your illusions. There is no longer a need for the ego to spin webs of illusions in order to maintain its false identity. The ego—in the way that you thought of and identified with it—is now transformed into a tool to be used by spirit. When you awaken to who you really are, the ego fades into the far recesses of your mind, back to the land of oblivion from which it arose. Its errant thought system has proven false.

In addition to giving up illusions at every stage of spiritual development, you will also have to give up illusions in the different areas of your life. In the area of your personal relationships there are many illusions to surrender. When you are in Egypt in your personal life, the illusions that assail you are the belief that you are without love, and that you need another to complete you, filling your lack. These illusions preoccupy you, compelling you to search outside yourself for the ego's illusory version of love. You will be led to challenge the illusion that with another in your life, the happiness that eludes you will become yours. This illusion of the ego asks you to believe that another holds the key to your happiness, and that happiness is something found outside of you. Before you are ready to give up these illusions that are deeply entrenched in your psyche, you must first discover for yourself if there is any truth to them.

You will soon find out, after being in relationship with another after a brief honeymoon period of three to six months, that it is not so easy to remain happy over a long period of time. This is especially true if you are dependent on the actions of another for your happiness. You are held captive by your emotions, which are triggered by the actions of someone other than yourself. You experience great joy, but also great sorrow and pain. How can happiness be experienced in this state of emotional seesawing? It cannot. The illusion that another holds the key to your happiness can only be found to be false after being in a relationship with another. If you do not allow yourself to be in a romantic relationship, the illusion of what it will offer you will remain deeply rooted in your psyche.

The truth that will take you out of bondage in Egypt in the area of personal relationships is realizing that happiness is something you give to yourself. The source of your happiness is a state of love found within you, and which you connect to on a regular basis. When you truly realize this, you must give up the ego's obsession with the notion of romantic love. The ego is addicted to the belief that love must be earned, worked for, and involves a struggle of some kind.

The purpose that your ego ascribes to personal relationships is another illusion that must be given up. In truth, you do not know the real

The Greatest Illusion

purpose of being in a relationship with another. Your ego has determined the purpose of all your relationships for you. It has created a belief that you are deficient in some way, and that the way to fill your deficiencies lies in seeking what you think you lack from another. Of course, you are not consciously aware how the ego is controlling your behavior. Instead you remain externally focused on obtaining what the ego believes is the purpose of personal relationships: acquiring love from a place outside yourself.

You leave the Egypt phase of spiritual development in the area of personal relationships when you can accept the truth that you do not receive love or happiness from another: you receive it from yourself. When you are ready to cross over the troubling sea of these revelations, but are not quite yet ready to fully surrender the ego's purpose for romantic relationships, you are in the Red Sea stage of spiritual development.

You enter the Wilderness phase when the pain associated with giving up your illusions becomes too much for you to bear alone. You will choose now to join in conscious union with God. In the Wilderness you bring on God as a partner in your romantic relationship. God now becomes a character in your drama, acting out the role you assigned him as supporter, confessor, and miracle worker. In the Wilderness, the notion that you are without love is heightened to the nth degree. Here you struggle with the pain of being cut off from an outer source of love. What you really have been cut off from up to now is authentic love, which is found inside of you. Instead you spent all your time looking for love outwardly, insisting that you knew where it was to be found.

You have become very attached to the illusion that your happiness—and your heart—remaining intact depend on the actions of another instead of yourself. You believe this—so much so that this illusion becomes an addiction of sorts. You also become addicted to the drama associated with the illusion. Instead of giving love to yourself, you prefer to enact dramas of trying to win it from others.

This results in you not receiving love: not only from yourself, but from others as well when they are in relationship with you, since they reflect your feelings of a lack of love back to you. Others in relationships act like mirrors reflecting our deepest fears; if you are projecting, "I want to be loved," then they will mirror back to you an experience of not being loved, as taught in *Conversations with God*. Why? Because your need to be loved is creating the effect opposite from what you desire. The truth is, you cannot experience with others what you do not first authentically obtain for yourself. No one can love you first, in order for you to follow suit.

In truth you lack nothing—especially love—but your ego does not believe this. So you disavow your soul by denying its existence, in order to fulfill the illusory desires of your heart as determined by the ego. You disavow your soul by giving up your true identity, and your beliefs, in order to be and remain with another. You seek another's approval in any way you can. This is the self-created drama you have come to associate with love of the romantic nature. Suffering becomes akin to love. Rejection becomes akin to love. Struggle becomes akin to love. In fact, love is none of those things—except to the ego.

The greatest illusion you are called to give up in the Wilderness is that you cannot happily exist without another in your life. In the Wilderness you may experience the end of some of your personal relationships as a result of your evolving consciousness. When you are separated from a beloved one's body, suffering from pangs of loneliness and grief, reach for God in the silence. The time you now spend alone, being with yourself, you will come to find satisfying. Acquiring the ability to be alone and in peace is a long and arduous process. How long you take to acquire a state of peace when alone will depend on the extent to which you are still attached to illusions.

The Greatest Illusion

This work may seem too painful, too hard to accomplish at first. It will not be surprising if you choose to quickly reengage in a new relationship—or an old one again—in avoidance of this challenging work. Doing this will cause you to repeat the same experiences and dramas anew. A deeply held illusion brings about the same predictable results. As we all know, the definition of insanity is doing the same action over and over again, expecting a different result.

Some of us choose never to awaken; we refuse to accept that our thoughts are the very things that make us slaves to illusions. These ego-filled thoughts keep us trapped in a vicious cycle, where our beliefs about ourselves are mirrored back to us through others who we are in relationships with. We cannot bear to face what giving up this illusion could mean. The ego has convinced us that accepting personal responsibility for loving ourselves means our bodies will remain alone indefinitely.

But illusions are not truth: an illusion is something created in place of the truth. The fear of being alone and without love is the main thing that prevents people from giving up illusions of the romantic sort. With the loss of a personal relationship, people fear they will never again find happiness, joy, or love. In fact it is quite the opposite: when a relationship comes to the point where you can no longer express unrestricted joy, peace, or love, it is time to move on. You can more easily reach these states of being in yourself when you are out of a relationship that limits your true expression as spirit.

One person alone cannot make a relationship work, no matter how spiritually developed one half of the relationship might be. Many women have yet to come to this realization; men tend to be more practical. The consciousness of one partner should ideally match the consciousness of the other. If this is not the case, at minimum the relationship should be supportive of the higher consciousness in the relationship. The person with the higher consciousness needs the freedom to express themselves without any resistance.

To choose to remain in a relationship past the point of growth is detrimental to one's spiritual evolution. The primary reason people choose to do so is fear of the unknown. Allow others simply to be where they are in consciousness. If this cannot be done comfortably while you are in a relationship, grant your partner the freedom to find another with whom they can unite in like-minded consciousness. You must let them go, wish them well, and move on. Someone who will share your current level of spiritual development awaits you as well.

This is not an easy thing to do, letting others go and moving on—it is quite challenging. You will find it hard to accept that another will not choose to come from the highest place within them when interacting with you in a relationship. But you must face the truth that most people find it easier to choose the lowest, easiest way—the path of least resistance—in life and in relationships. They go with what feels comfortable, good, and right at the time, regardless of whether they are capable of experiencing something higher. It is far easier for them to come from a place of ego. The easiest choice is to be with another who reflects their ego's level of consciousness; this enables them to avoid any inner work necessary to consciously evolve. I observe that this behavior in relationships is more readily found in men. This is not an indictment—merely an observation.

When you have let go of a personal relationship that was no longer serving your highest good, you are in the Jordan River stage of spiritual development. In the Jordan River you will have to do challenging inner work on a daily basis. While it is true that the Jordan River stage is synonymous with outer work, the outer work you will be doing here is to withstand outside stimuli that suggest there is something wrong with you because you are not in a relationship. You will be bombarded with these stimuli on a daily basis in the outer world. One, in human terms, is deemed a lonely number. In spiritual terms, one is seen as *completion*.

This is not to say that you will not be with others in the Jordan River. Your *body* is what may not be with another during this stage. You will be with the sum of all of your parts, your spirit, and in turn with the spirit of others. Those of us who cannot be at peace without being in a relationship need to honestly ask ourselves an important question. Is being in a relationship really that much better, that much happier? If your answer is yes, then ask yourself who is really answering the question: your ego or your spirit? We also need to determine what it is we dislike about ourselves that prevents us from wanting to spend time alone with ourselves for very long. Remember: the self being referred to is your spirit, not your ego—how many of us would want to spend time with our ego?

Limiting self-beliefs must be challenged and eradicated from our consciousness without delay. To those who can be alone with themselves, but do not necessarily find it enjoyable, there is more inner work that still needs to be done. You must develop a higher awareness of yourself as spirit, and reap the benefits that come from knowing yourself as such. In the Jordan River you are called to give up the illusion of romantic love as defined by the ego and by society. You must now come from a spiritual perspective of what love is and where it is to be found.

Love is not dependent on another in any way, shape, or form. You can love another without having met them—for instance, a grandparent who passed on before you were born. You can also love another who is no longer in your physical life, such as a person who has made their Earthly transition. This proves that the illusion you believe in—that the absence of a beloved's body means you can no longer experience the love that you feel for them—is false. Love is not experienced merely because two *bodies* are together. Real love—not the false ego version—is experienced between *spirits*. You do not need a body in order to remain in relationship with others whom you love; you are connected in spirit. Allow their body to leave yours in peace when the time comes. Bodies are often distractions to the authentic expression of love. They are seen as the object of love, instead of a person's spirit.

If you are in a relationship with another and you must part ways, know that you are not losing the love you experience with them. Bodies rarely choose to stay together for a lifetime, though hearts sometimes do. The choice to remain in a place of love through an internal, spiritual connection with another is available. Do not mourn the departure of the body of a loved one. Connect to a form of love that is still available for you to express. This is not done by invoking memories of past experiences, but by connecting on an inner plane with the essence of the spirit of the one you love.

When you are connected to your spirit in conscious remembrance of those you love, you can still feel their presence, and they can feel yours. Thus, outer communication among individuals is not always necessary. In fact, it would be good for some of you to break off outer communications with others in your life, even for a little while. Silence is not a bad thing; it is a healing thing at times. Allow yourself to be liberated from the notion that you need another's physical presence in your life in order to continue loving them.

You will arrive at the Promised Land state of spiritual development when you come to accept that love is the very essence and nature of who you are. You can no more be without love than you can be without air on Earth. Love surrounds you and emanates from within you; it is part of the essence of who you are. You are made out of love, and you *are* love. There is no way possible to be without love; you suffer acutely when you do not know this.

To feel love, all you have to do is take a deep breath and go inside. The sensation that rises up within you when you are connected to your spirit through breathing is one of love. If you do not experience a feeling of love after taking a breath and stilling your mind, take several more deep breaths. This will connect you to the place of love inside you.

How love should look and where it can be found are the illusions you must give up in order to enter the Promised Land in this area. In the Promised Land you are no longer seeking love outside yourself—in fact, you are quite sure it cannot be found outside yourself. However, the lingering attachments to illusions you once held must be eliminated in consciousness. The ego will seek to draw relationship scenarios to you that reflect your old pattern of looking for love outside of yourself. You must shut these attempts down and see them for what they are: the ego's refusal to accept truth in place of illusion.

In the Promised Land you must cultivate a relationship with your higher, true self. Pursuing the agenda of your spirit will bring about a sense of fulfillment and accomplishment within. You will come to know that you are not without love. You now know where it is to be found: within.

This is not to say you will not engage in a meaningful relationship with anyone—but it will no longer be with the purpose of acquiring love. Instead, the purpose becomes to have an outer experience of the love you feel for yourself when in a relationship with others. Romantic relationships then become a tool for self-growth and self-reflection, with these relationships serving as a mirror to your inner feelings about yourself.

How can you reevaluate the purpose of romantic relationships from a spiritual perspective?

24

What Is It for Me to Do?

THE WORK THAT NOW HAS to be done in your consciousness is giving up what will prevent your spiritual evolution. In the area of your professional life, you are in Egypt when your goal for working is simply to make money. Working a standard workweek at a routine job brings its own reward: a paycheck. Egypt is the place where you finance your material comforts. You use your salary to buy things such as a house, a car, clothes, trips, jewelry, electronics, and other material items. When you are still preoccupied with your basic survival needs, you are in Egypt. When you are actively engaged in acquiring an education, titles, promotions, and an office, this is an indication that you are still in Egypt. You are also in Egypt when you have settled for the practical version of your passion in the area of work. When you cannot even recall what your spirit passionately desires to do, you are in Egypt.

Being in Egypt is not a bad thing; in fact, survival is a necessary thing. Knowing where you are in consciousness is what is important.

You will be ready to leave Egypt when the survival of your body is no longer your most dominant preoccupation. You must be ready to give up the illusion of financial security which a regular paycheck provides. Awareness of your emerging soul now becomes your primary area of focus. The longings of your soul will become louder than societal conditioning, even stronger than the fear inside you. You will resist the spiritual nudging taking place inside you for as long as you can. Your soul is urging you to take a journey.

Most people have been so successful, for so long, at drowning out the voice of their soul and its passions that it will take a long time to reconnect with that voice. Even after the connection has been reestablished, many will still choose to ignore its guidance; they lack the courage to go in search of the unknown. The reason most people do not live the highest possible vision of their life is because, in order to do so, they must do challenging inner work. Doing this inner work will bring about profound changes in one's outer life.

Once and for all, let us dispel the belief that people cannot change. This is no longer an acceptable excuse; they must now do something to actively change their lives for the better.

The journey of the soul calls for you to challenge the belief that you are what you possess. A lot of people prefer to remain where they are in consciousness—and they do so knowing that they are not having a joyful experience of life. They are willing to settle for mediocrity. For most of you, this is enough; the god of mediocrity pays well. You believe that your present existence is the best that life can offer you. You are unwilling to rock the steady course of the life you are following. Safety and predictability are some of the other gods you serve.

But serving the gods you made in the ego's image will eventually bring you to a place of extreme discontent with your life. This discontent may lead you to make alcohol, food, drugs, illness—or any other means of denial you choose—into the new god you worship. The purpose of this new god is to deny the acute feeling of pain and a sense that something irreplaceable is lost.

What you have lost, that you use other means to cope with, is a connection with your spirit. Without your spirit you can never feel whole. So the question to ask yourself is not so much, "Should I move?" as much as, "What am I giving up by remaining still?" The answer is, "I am giving up myself—my true self, that is." Is the value of your soul not worth taking into consideration? Or is it easier to remain stuck and afraid? To most of you, the answer to the second question is, "Yes. It is far easier for me to do nothing, and to remain exactly where I am."

Still, some will be unable to resist the urgings of their soul. The more they become in tune with it, the more intensely their soul will reverberate in them, until they are unable to deny its presence. When you cross over the Red Sea of fearful thoughts about making a change in your life, you make the decision to take the journey of the soul. This leap of faith brings you to the border of the Wilderness stage of spiritual development.

In the Wilderness, you will be called to give up the illusion that you are truly alone in life. Although you will experience a great deal of solitude in this stage of development, be assured that the I Am is with you. The comforter awaits your recognition. God becomes a deep and meaningful presence, active in your life and affairs. God will become your confidante, friend, confessor, but most of all he will become known to you in a real and tangible way. His presence, which you deeply connect with, will force you to give up the illusion—once and for all—that you are alone in the world.

In this stage of development you will also give up the illusion that money comes from anywhere other than your internal connection to the divine. God sends you sustenance through a host of miraculous means; this sustenance will sustain you during your long stay in the Wilderness. You will learn not to depend on familiar ways of obtaining money, and one dollar in the Wilderness will seem like a lot of money. Your appreciation for the way the Universe provides for you during this stage will lead you to a place of radical faith and trust in the Lord. God will use other people as a means to provide you with sustenance. Others may not enjoy being used in this way, but their own souls will evolve as a result of their generosity. Who knows when it may be their turn to benefit from your generosity, when they embark on their own journeys of the soul?

The greatest illusion you will give up is the one that asks you to believe that you are an ego. You will lose all identification with the ego and its preoccupations as being real. A new you—as spirit—will be born. Your old way of thinking, based on the dictates of the ego, will be transformed into a higher way of thinking, now based on spirit.

Your spirit will long to be of service in the world, because it will no longer be in service to its own ego. The desire to serve will propel you to seek work again in the outer world. It will also help you surrender the ego's need to feel important and have material status. The work you initially do will be of a humbling nature, and you will often feel confused about how your life is unfolding. This confusion will stem from the transformative process you are undergoing: you are changing from a lower state of being to a higher one. The best thing you can do for yourself is to observe the changes you are going through, without judging them.

When it is time to leave the Wilderness, you will be led to the place where you can be of most service at this particular juncture in your life. You will have learned the true source of your abundance. You will never feel alone again because your relationship with the I Am will remain steadfast, a constant presence in your life. The Wilderness is where you will shed most of the illusions you hold about the world. You will adopt spiritual truth in place of Earthly illusions.

In the Jordan River stage in the area of work, you will give up the illusion that there is anything in life you cannot accomplish. When you are in the Jordan, your belief in your limitations will be challenged. Your fears will manifest in your physical reality in order for you to eradicate them in your consciousness. You will persevere by sheer hard work and faith in the I Am. You will give up the illusion that fear can prevent you from moving forward. Conquering your fear becomes an alchemic process in the Jordan River phase: the lower energy of fear is transmuted into the higher energies of faith and courage.

Reaching the Promised Land stage in the area of work will seem anticlimactic after your struggles in the Jordan River, but the Promised Land has its own set of challenges. You will struggle with remaining areas in your consciousness that need divine healing: mainly issues of your worth. Acquiring a high degree of self-esteem is a goal you must accomplish in the Promised Land. By not knowing your true worth and your spiritual identity, you prevent yourself from using the spiritual gifts bequeathed to you by the I Am. God bestows spiritual gifts upon each of us; when not used or denied over a long period of time, these gifts become difficult to access. To deny your worth is to deny the worth of God—after all, did not the I Am create you in "his own image and likeness"?

You may have doubts about yourself. Do you doubt God's opinion about you as well? All that you create and accomplish on Earth serves as testimony to his existence. We glorify God by accepting our worth, our gifts, and by using them in the world. Those who witness your achievements behold the spirit of God in you. When others praise your accomplishments, what they are truly saying is, "great is God, the

Creator of all." If you do not like your own image, focus on God; the I Am will help you see that his image and yours are one and the same.

God did not create anything on Earth that has no worth. Even ants serve a divine purpose and have worth. Are we not at least as worthy as an ant? If God had a purpose in mind for ants, will he not have one in mind for you? The purpose of ants is to remind us that bigger things can be carried on the backs of things that are the smallest and appear weakest in nature. How many things have you carried on your back that seemed too large and impossible for you to carry? Is it not interesting to note and marvel at the strength of our friends in nature?

The difference between animals and us is that animals do not question their worth or place in life. Why do we? Why are we so chronically afraid that we are unworthy of our good? In the Promised Land you will have the opportunity to develop a higher opinion of yourself and learn your worth.

When you have transcended in consciousness all 31 sublevels of lower-level thought systems, you will reach Christ Consciousness. Your work will then take on universal importance. You will work to uplift humanity, and help others to awaken to their divinity as well. Your work on Earth will be completed when you have accomplished your spiritual mission given to you by the I Am.

COMPASS

What are your spiritual gifts?

25

Cultivating a Self-Relationship

ONCE YOU HAVE CONQUERED YOUR outer surroundings, you are now ready to conquer yourself. The journey of the soul is about conquering what keeps you from coming to know the *real* you. The journey is taken with the purpose of reconnecting with oneself—from the inside out. This journey does not begin until you have lost interest in outer pursuits. The best time to start this journey is when you have awoken from your beliefs in illusions. You are quite lucid now, having learned a valuable lesson: what you seek cannot be found outside you. Now you must head into the depths of your own being, relating to yourself in a way you never have before.

The ego does not want to venture inside; it knows this will end its false dominance over your mind. Its only chance for continued survival is

Cultivating a Self-Relationship

remaining focused on the outer world, since only in the outer world is the ego made real. The first major barrier you face after venturing inside is your greatest fear that you are alone and will always be so. Is that not why you tried so hard to find love outside yourself? You now know you are not without love, but the fear that you are alone still lingers. The ego requires an audience. "Who am I if there is nobody there to see me?" it asks. Alone is the last thing that the ego wants to be—who will serve as witness to its existence? Spirit needs no such witness.

It is now time to give up the illusion of being alone once and for all; it is incorrect. Others being with your body does not make you any less alone than when you are with yourself. You can feel just as alone in the company of others as when you are only with yourself—sometimes even more so. While others may provide companionship, that is different from an end to loneliness. The end to loneliness is realizing you are never alone.

Your spirit within you is connected to the source of all: God. You are a part of God. If you are a part of all, how can you also be alone? The dread of being alone has caused humans to make choices out of fear instead of self-love. I will repeat: the body of another in close proximity to yours does not make you any less alone. It may offer you an *illusion* that loneliness has ended, but it is just that: an illusion. It is up to you to realize your unity with the divine.

God does not wish for you to be alone. He has created life in such a way that if you truly sought out the truth, you would realize that being alone is quite impossible. Your spirit is a divine aspect of God expressing as you; it is a constant companion, and always with you. Spirit expands exponentially and has no end.

Once again, your spirit is connected to a larger one; this larger spirit is God. If you are part of this larger spirit, how can you ever find yourself alone? You can declare, "I am not aware of my higher self, and thus my connection to the unified spirit has been temporarily suspended." It is only temporary—at any moment you have the power to reconnect to the divine within. All that is needed is a willingness to do so.

When you are feeling alone, it is your spirit's way of saying, "hey, look at me—over here!" Your spirit is trying to get your attention. You answer its call by looking outside yourself to fulfill your desire for companionship. But your spirit is calling you to serve as your companion—will you not heed its call? You need go no further than inside yourself to gain companionship. With this union will come an even greater one: a relationship with God.

You may wonder how one makes this connection. It is actually quite simple: when you are feeling lonely and alone in life, connect to the source inside. You do this by silencing all thoughts, allowing the love within you to rise up and make its presence known. Love feels like a stimulating force within. As you go deeper into this awareness, you will connect to an even higher presence in the silence. That will be the presence of God. The realization of both of these presences—your spirit and God's—will not allow you to keep clinging to the illusion of being alone. For you can never be alone: God is always with you.

Many of us, however, will not choose to make this connection. Instead, we choose to persist in believing that God cannot be known to us in any meaningful way. Most of the time you spend on Earth, you will spend alone—it is a simple fact. Learning to make peace with being alone is a necessary step in maturing spiritually. Your soul seeks to learn from its experiences; how many times have you given it experiences of despair about feeling alone?

There is another choice, but few will make it: the choice for your spirit. Is your spirit a physical presence in your life? No, but that does not mean it has nothing valuable to offer you. Allow your spirit to comfort you during the times you feel alone. You must experience loneliness before you can begin to transcend this state. A delay in starting the soul's journey in the life area of relationship with yourself will leave you stuck believing in illusions for an indefinite period of time.

How God aches for the pain you feel due to your self-imposed feelings of separation! You do not even know what it is you are separated from: the power and presence of God in your life. Real separation occurs when you abandon your connection with the I Am—not from the separation of physical bodies. At least know what you are truly longing for: complete reunion with God. What you long for also longs for you—the I Am yearns to be with you, and to connect with you in love. Since you do not know how to remove the barriers that separate you from the I Am, God must work through you to remove these barriers.

The first impediment that must be removed is the thought that God is not enough. God is all that there is. How can *all* not be enough? The ego rejects this truth, because it does not meet the ego's criteria for fulfillment. But you are not the ego. Your authentic identity has been given to you through reunion with your spirit.

We are part of God, and to join with God in conscious union makes us aware that we are a fraction of the whole of existence. This is not a frivolous thing. Do not throw your inheritance lightly away: it is the "Kingdom of God" you are inheriting. On Earth, the only kingdom you are interested in is a kingdom of illusions. Illusions are not real—so why persist in believing they have something valuable to offer? They have nothing to offer you, except a way to show you where the answer does not lie.

If you know where the answer does not lie, why do you persist in looking there? Is it because you still refuse to accept the fact that the answer does not lie where you prefer? Your stubbornness and resistance to the truth will only delay your own healing. You are indefinitely keeping your wounds, caused by choosing illusions over truth, from healing. Why cause yourself continual, unnecessary pain?

Is it so difficult to accept that real love and companionship is found only in God? Instead of saddening you, this should uplift you. Truth brings about liberation—you no longer need to beg for love, or feel you have to be clever enough to keep others around you, in order to maintain it. You need no longer feel "less than" merely because you are not in a romantic relationship.

Why is truth not preferable to illusion? Maybe it is because you know that when your last illusion is gone, there remains nothing left to hide behind. Journeying into the unchartered waters of your soul frightens you. Delay no more: unhappiness is too high a price to continue paying out of a sheer lack of gumption. You must be brave and agree to venture inside yourself.

It is only here that the real journey begins. You are led to leave Egypt, cross over the Red Sea, wander in the Wilderness, go through the Jordan River, and enter into the Promised Land before evolving into Christ Consciousness. This is the blueprint for your spiritual evolution on Earth.

You are in Egypt when you are not even aware that what you seek can be found only through a relationship with yourself. You are ready to cross over the Red Sea when you are willing to cease all outer attempts to find fulfillment other than an authentic relationship with yourself. Your sea of emotions of limited, illusory thinking has held you in bondage long enough. The only option left is to venture inside.

After you have made the decision to do so, you will enter the Wilderness stage of spiritual development. This is the place where a relationship with yourself can now take place. You will find yourself in a period of silence and solitude. You will initially resist these states, and wish you were anywhere but here. You will also replay memories of past relationships with others, hoping to still feel connected to someone other than yourself.

Up until now, you have used your mind to keep you in constant contact with the outside world by way of your thoughts. Your mind's new role will be connecting to that which is inside of you: your spirit. This can be accomplished now only by the *absence* of thoughts.

In the Wilderness stage, in the area of cultivating a relationship with yourself, you will learn about—and start to use—the gifts of your spirit. Spiritual gifts are inherent, but how they are expressed through you is unique in nature. Many people have similar gifts, but no two gifts are expressed in the same way—each expression of the divine is distinct. It is up to you to decide when (or even if) you should use your spiritual gifts. They are there, inside of you, ready to tap into whenever you decide. These spiritual gifts are seeds, planted within you by the divine. Whether or not these seeds will germinate and blossom into a rich bounty of harvest called your life depends solely on you.

What message are you sending to God by not using your spiritual gifts? You may doubt your own divine abilities, but do you doubt God's as well? Or do you merely doubt that God's gifts can come through you? Doubt no more! God's gifts are just that: gifts given to you by him, to be expressed through you. In receiving his gifts and choosing to use them, you glorify and honor the Creator of all. Have you ever considered your gifts in this way—that using them honors God? This is, in fact, what you are doing when you allow your splendor to seep out of you, into expression in the world.

Live your passion. Your passion is simply the thing you have always wanted to do with your life: your secret dream of dreams. Make your dreams secret no more. Secrets are for those unwilling to allow in the light of truth. The light of truth is that which longs to be expressed through you—it was given to you to do just that. Most people do not pursue their passion because they doubt their ability to accomplish their dreams. While you may doubt *your* ability to succeed, do not doubt your *spirit's* ability to do so.

In the Wilderness you will get past the fearful thoughts in your mind; you will discover and finally use the gifts of your spirit. When you begin to use these gifts, you enter into the Jordan River stage of spiritual development. Here you will have to do the work necessary to bring about the manifestation of your dreams in the outer world. Each day you will be called upon to tackle or transcend your fears. When you take your mind out of the equation, you will accomplish great things.

It is in you to accomplish great things, for the I Am does not seek smallness. What is the purpose of "hiding your light under a bushel"? Light must shine by its very nature. You must become aware of the light of spirit within you. You will then serve as an example to others, encouraging them to stoke the embers of their own lights within. It is never too late to accomplish your heart's desires. Being too old is not an excuse, yet it is one the ego attempts to use quite often.

The success you will achieve in the Jordan River will not satisfy the ego's definition of success, which is based on the material. Your spirit will define success as the joy you will feel in creating. Each time you create, you connect that much more with your spirit, and you experience a little more of your true and whole self. In the long run, spirit will not be denied, but it can be temporarily delayed—by the resistant efforts of your mind. Not indefinitely, though: spirit's wishes will eventually be realized—if not in this lifetime, then in another.

Your spirit is now ready to become known to you; it has waited a long time for this homecoming. You will come into conscious contact with your spirit, and its beauty will humble you. You do not have to do anything difficult for this union to take place; the only requirement is a willingness to make contact and look inside yourself for all you seek. Spirit will do the rest.

Spirit does not speak in terms you will understand; it operates in the form of vibrations. The spirit within you can be felt as a vibration radiating peace and love. Its presence is subtle at first, until you begin to merge more fully with it. You will feel a profound sense of returning home. Spirit will fill up the empty spaces within you. When you can operate from a place of spirit and still engage in outer work in the world without breaking your connection to spirit, you will be ready to leave the Wilderness stage of development.

It will be challenging to maintain this connection to spirit—everything has the potential to break it when you engage in activity in the outer world. The thoughts you hold in your mind, now outwardly focused again, are what will potentially alienate you from your spirit. They will attempt to make you believe again in the illusion that you are your body and your human personality.

To list all the possible distractions to your mind is impossible. What you need to know is this: silencing your mind and maintaining an open connection to your spirit is imperative. Even in the midst of the three-dimensional physical illusions that surround you, keep your mind silent. If you do, you will experience no interference with the signal you receive from your spirit.

You are connected to spirit by a wave of vibrations; the higher the rate of your vibration, the more spirit you resonate. How does this process work? You can be at your job, fully engaged in work, yet at the same time your mind is free of thoughts, thus keeping open the connection to spirit.

Do you think you need your mind in order to perform physical functions in your life? You do not. In fact, when you do not use the mind for decision-making, things turn out better. This is because you are not using your mind to doubt that anything you want to do can be accomplished. You also waste no time mulling over what accomplishing the things you desire will mean. You act from a higher place when you engage your spirit instead of your mind.

Spirit acts from a place of pure knowingness. Often you experience doubt when this happens, because it threatens the order of things established by your mind. Do you want to experience an extraordinary life? Then stop living through your mind and thoughts—instead, experience life through the wisdom of your *spirit*.

When you live life in this way, you can call on spiritual resources to aid you in creating your ideal life. Spirit is creative in nature; thus, creating comes easy to it. There can be no easier job than creating with your spirit. What often makes this job seem tedious and impossible is that you factor the mind into it. The mind has the opposite effect: it seeks to slow down creativity, offering in its place fear, indecision, doubt, and resistance to what is.

When you cultivate a close relationship with your spirit, and identify with it as being you, then you will have reached the Promised Land stage of spiritual development. Next, you will travel through 31 sublevels in consciousness. In each sublevel, another layer of your lower consciousness is peeled away. When you reach the core of your spiritual identity, you will experience yourself as being divine. You will have obtained the Christ Consciousness level of spiritual development.

COMPASS

How can you create a life full of extraordinary experiences?

26

Why Take the Journey?

WHAT CAN BE THE PURPOSE of such a laborious journey? Is it merely for the journey itself? What is a journey without the experiences we gain along the way? The journey of your soul seems to stretch out before you: seemingly with no end in sight. Discovery for its own sake is as futile as a journey that reaches nowhere.

The purpose of the journey of the soul is to progress in consciousness through successive stages in spiritual development. One must exit Egypt, cross over the Red Sea, wander in the Wilderness, go through the Jordan River, and arrive in the Promised Land. Ultimately, this journey will lead us to discover our true identity as the Christ.

The journey of the soul will enable you to experience the highest aspects of your consciousness. You will attain that which you have always sought: happiness, joy, peace, prosperity, good health, and a sense of fulfillment. These gifts of spirit are a byproduct of the journey; you receive them when you reach the Promised Land.

These gifts are not in themselves the means to the end, except maybe to the ego. The means to the end for your spirit is an awareness of yourself as God. There can be no higher recompense. Spirit finds fulfillment through the act of creating. How much you create is up to you—but creating is the goal of your spirit. In this way it too has the experience of being God.

Claim your inheritance as a child of God: sit with Christ on the right hand of the altar of the Almighty, with all the others who have reached the journey's end. What does this mean in practical terms? We know scientifically that one cell in a body has the same composition as the entire body, just on a smaller scale. So each individual cell is a composite of, and is as capable as, the whole body. Imagine yourself as a single cell in the body of God. This makes you one with God, part of God, and God in your own right—all at the same time.

It does not matter what you call yourself. Nothing can change the truth that within you is the same composite of the genetic code found in the Universe and in God.

The question that remains is: what are you going to do with this knowledge? Will you claim your inheritance—or will you deny this truth and instead argue for your limitations? For those ready to accept your true place in existence, delay no more and begin your journey of the soul. To those who are not quite ready to begin the journey, at least be knowledgeable about what it entails, so you will be prepared when you are ready to take it.

When you are ready to accept your divine inheritance, a divine reward will be waiting for you: the experience of yourself as the Creator. The journey of the soul awaits you, my friend.

Why should you take the journey of the soul?

Poem - The Journey

The journey takes place inside of me.
I travel to unknown lands and visit sites never seen before.
I journey, you see, to reach locations that exist inside of me.
I used to fear this journey, that of my unknown self, and put it off indefinitely.
But the time came when the distant shores outside no longer interested me.
So I followed my compass of intuition, heading in a new direction, one leading deep inside of me.
This is the journey I was born to take and am led by spirit to consciously undertake.

To conquer the many lands that lie inside me,
I first must venture through a valley named fear whose domain seems endless in sight.

In this abyss lie doubts, lack of self-worth, and places with names similar in scope.
I challenge these shadowy thoughts with conviction, giving over my power to them no more.
As I journey through this barren wasteland in my mind,
I find the strength to persevere, having overcome the shadows that once made me quiver in their wake.
Liberated, I trek on triumphantly to places never imagined within me.

The journey is a lonely one, since I am the only one who can journey inside.
I travel bravely alone on my quest to reach unfamiliar lands.
Where the journey will end, I do not know.
I cannot rest at one location for too long because of inner urgings that are sure to arise,

Creating in their wake a restless spirit within,
Alerting me that the time has come again to journey to higher ground.
Each level of land I ascend strengthens me,
Prepares me for what awaits me in the lands I am yet to cross.
I am on a journey through the depths of my soul.

The call to journey has sounded.
I arise and permit fear to delay me no more.
For you see, I am ready. I now recognize
That the time is come to begin the journey with alacrity,
A journey whose locations are deep inside me.
I am on the journey of the soul.

From the Author

WHO AM I? From a spiritual perspective, I am one who sought to understand, always asking the question "why?" of God. I particularly wanted to know why we humans have to suffer so greatly while on Earth. I wanted to understand in an attempt to end my own suffering.

What followed was a journey, over 20 years, to seek answers. I have gained some understanding, and I have a lot more to acquire. What I do know for sure is this: we are souls on a journey of spiritual development on Earth. Each stage of this journey has specific lessons we must learn, and areas to reach in consciousness in order to evolve spiritually. That is why in this book I repeat central concepts over and over again, so that they can become firmly rooted in your consciousness.

Understanding what spiritual stage of development I am in—in every area of my life—and knowing what is required to evolve higher in consciousness has helped me tremendously. It has allowed me to understand that my life is not just a series of random events: there is a divine order to it. I have a blueprint for the journey of the soul that I can follow, and doing so will help make evolving easier.

I share my journey with you in hopes that it will help me to continue evolving spiritually. Also, that it will offer you insight and guidance on your own journey of the soul. I am currently working on *Resistance is Key*, a book on how to remove inner resistance to the good that we desire to manifest.

By sharing we learn from each other. Knowledge is the key to understanding, understanding is the key to achieving, and achieving is the key to becoming.

From a personal perspective: I have been a Marylander for my entire life. I love to travel internationally. I have a Master's Degree in Education and a Bachelor's of Arts degree with a specialization in Journalism and the Humanities.

Authors are dependent on our readers to get the word out about our books, especially spiritual ones! If *Compass: The Journey of the Soul from Egypt to the Promised Land* has resonated with you, then I ask you to please write a review (no matter how brief) on Amazon.com. I appreciate your support!

My sincere intention is for you to reach your Promised Land in every area of your life.

Namaste,
Penelope

Staying Connected

CONTINUE YOUR JOURNEY OF THE SOUL at:

www.penelopeyorke.com

Sign up for the *Compass Newsletter* to receive information on: book releases, e-courses, read articles, and to stay connected on the journey of your soul.

You will receive a <u>FREE</u> download of the *Compass Companion eWorkbook* (Interactive PDF format) as a thank-you gift for signing up.

The *Compass Companion Workbook* provides further insight into every stage of spiritual development; offers reflection questions, and gives you a place to answer those questions. It also contains spiritual activities, and a planner to organize these activities. The print version of the workbook (ISBN 978-0-9863896-0-3) is available at Amazon.com.

Applying key concepts from the book *Compass,* and doing necessary follow-up work is a tool for you to use in evolving. I invite you to take *Compass Interactive Courses* in your own home at a pace you set.

To take these courses visit:
www.pcsresources.education/

Follow the *Compass Blog* at: **http://penelopeyorke.net/** for continuing insight and dialogue as a fellow traveler on the journey of the soul. You can also follow the *Compass Blog* by email, RSS feed, or on Kindle.

Compass Reflection Journals are available for each stage of spiritual development at Amazon.com. Each journal includes:

- A fillable Table of Contents
- Page Numbers
- 150 lined pages (75 sheets) *and* 30 unlined pages (15 sheets)
- Calendars for two years
- Reflection Questions and Activities
- Measurements: (large journal) 7 inches width x 9 inches height
- Flower and leaf motif design on every page

Visit **PCS Resources Store** at: www.penelopeyorke.com to purchase inspirational products containing quotes from *Compass* .

Notes

CHAPTER 1

[1] Charles Fillmore, Metaphysical Bible Dictionary, 183. (Unity Village, MO: Unity, 1995).

[2] Fillmore, Metaphysical Bible Dictionary, 183.

[3] Fillmore, Metaphysical Bible Dictionary, 183.

[4] Fillmore, Metaphysical Bible Dictionary, 520.

CHAPTER 3

[1] Neale Donald Walsch, Conversations with God, Books 1, 2, and 3 (Charlottesville, VA: Hampton Roads, 1995, 2002, 2003).

CHAPTER 4
[1] Dan Schutte, "Here I Am, Lord" (Portland, OR: OCP Publications, 1981).

CHAPTER 6
[1] Fillmore, Metaphysical Bible Dictionary, 364.
[2] Fillmore, Metaphysical Bible Dictionary, 365.
[3] Fillmore, Metaphysical Bible Dictionary, 368.

CHAPTER 7
[1] *A Course in Miracles*, T-1.I. (Mill Valley, CA: Foundation for Inner Peace; 2nd edition, 1992).

CHAPTER 8
[1] Fillmore, Metaphysical Bible Dictionary, 138.
[2] Fillmore, Metaphysical Bible Dictionary, 339.
[3] Fillmore, Metaphysical Bible Dictionary, 183.

CHAPTER 12
[1] Jim Marion, *Putting on the Mind of Christ* (Newburyport, MA: Hampton Roads, 2000).
[2] Eckhart Tolle, *The Power of Now* (**Novato, CA**: New World Library, 1999).
[3] Don Miguel Ruiz, *The Mastery of Love* (San Rafael, CA: Amber-Allen Publishing, 1999).

CHAPTER 15
[1] Fillmore, Metaphysical Bible Dictionary, 368.
[2] Fillmore, Metaphysical Bible Dictionary, 136.
[3] Eugene H. Peterson, *The Message//REMIX: The Bible in Contemporary Language.* (Colorado Springs, CO: NavPress, 2003), *Joshua* 4: 1-9.

[4] Charles Roth, *A Twelve-Power Meditation Exercise* (Unity Village, MO: Unity Press, 1989).

[5] Charles Fillmore and Cora Fillmore, *The Twelve Powers* (Unity Village, MO: Unity School of Christianity, 1999).

CHAPTER 16

[1] Fillmore, Metaphysical Bible Dictionary, 364.

[2] A Course in Miracles, W-pI.196.5:1.

[3] Wayne Dyer, *10 Secrets for Success and Inner Peace*, 21 (Carlsbad, CA: Hay House Inc., 2002).

[4] Dyer, 10 Secrets for Success and Inner Peace, 31.

[5] A Course in Miracles, T-4.I.7:1,2,3.

CHAPTER 19

[1] Peterson, The Message//REMIX: The Bible in Contemporary Language, Luke 23:34.

[2] Peterson, The Message//REMIX: The Bible in Contemporary Language, Psalms 23:4.

CHAPTER 21

[1] Peterson, The Message//REMIX: The Bible in Contemporary Language, Exodus 3:8.

[2] Peterson, The Message//REMIX: The Bible in Contemporary Language, Luke 2:49-50.

[3] Peterson, The Message//REMIX: The Bible in Contemporary Language, Matthew 27:46.

Bibliography

A Course in Miracles. Mill Valley, CA: Foundation for Inner Peace, 1992.

Wayne Dyer. *10 Secrets for Success and Inner Peace*. Carlsbad, CA: Hay House, 2002.

Charles Fillmore. *Metaphysical Bible Dictionary*. Unity Village, Missouri: Unity, 1995.

Charles Fillmore and Cora Fillmore. *The Twelve Powers*. Unity Village, MO: Unity School of Christianity, 1999.

Jim Marion. *Putting on the Mind of Christ*. Newburyport, MA: Hampton Roads, 2000.

Eugene H. Peterson. *The Message//REMIX: The Bible in Contemporary Language*. Colorado Springs, CO: NavPress, 2003.

Dan Schutte. "Here I Am, Lord." Portland, OR: OCP Publications, 1981.

Charles Roth. *A Twelve-Power Meditation Exercise*. Unity Village, MO: Unity, 1989.

Bibliography

Don Miguel Ruiz. *The Mastery of Love.* San Rafael, CA: Amber-Allen Publishing, 1999.

Eckhart Tolle. *The Power of Now.* Novato, CA: New World Library, 1999.

Neale Donald Walsch. *Conversations with God, Books 1, 2, and 3.* Charlottesville, VA: Hampton Roads, 1995, 2002, 2003.

Stay Connected:

http://www.penelopeyorke.com (Author Website)

http://penelopeyorke.net/ (Blog)

http://www.pcsresources.education/ (*Compass* Courses)

http://www.zazzle.com/pcsresources (PCS Store)

https://twitter.com/PenelopeYorke (Twitter)

https://www.pinterest.com/pcsresources (Pinterest)

www.ingramcontent.com/pod-product-compliance
Lightning Source LLC
Chambersburg PA
CBHW030438300426
44112CB00009B/1065